Classics Canada

Authentic Readings for ESL Students

Patricia Brock
Dawson College

Brian John Busby

D1463753

Prentice Hall Regents Canada
Scarborough, Ontario

Canadian Cataloguing in Publication Data

Brock, Patricia
  Classics Canada

ISBN 0–13–328972–9

1. English language — Textbooks for second language learners.* 2. Readers — Canadian literature (English).* 3. Canadian literature (English).* I. Busby, Brian John II. Title.

PE1128.B76   1994   428.6'4   C94–931805–1

© 1995 Prentice-Hall Canada Inc., Scarborough, Ontario

ALL RIGHTS RESERVED
No part of this book may be reproduced in any form without permission in writing from the publisher.

Prentice-Hall, Inc., Englewood Cliffs, New Jersey
Prentice-Hall International (UK) Limited, London
Prentice-Hall of Australia, Pty. Limited, Sydney
Prentice-Hall Hispanoamericana, S.A., Mexico City
Prentice-Hall of India Private Limited, New Delhi
Prentice-Hall of Japan, Inc., Tokyo
Simon & Schuster Asia Private Limited, Singapore
Editora Prentice-Hall do Brasil, Ltda., Rio de Janeiro

ISBN 0–13–328972–9

Acquisitions: Cliff Newman
Managing Editor: Marta Tomins
Copy Editor: Becky Vogan
Production Editor: Imogen Brian
Production Coordinator: Anita Boyle
Photo Research: Karen Taylor
Cover Design and Page Layout: Gail Ferreira Ng-A-Kien
Cover Art: Brian Marion (Courtesy Gallery Louise Smith)

   2 3 4 5 W 99 98 97

Printed and bound in Canada

Every reasonable effort has been made to obtain permissions for all articles and data used in this edition. If errors or omissions have occurred, they will be corrected in future editions provided written notification has been received by the publisher.

To Helen Brock and Pauline Busby
All our love and affection
From Pat and Brian

Table of Contents

Acknowledgements

We are grateful to the following copyright holders for permission to reproduce and record the following texts:

"Loup-Garou" from *Legendary Creatures/ Créatures Légendaires* 1990. Courtesy of Canada Post Corporation, Ottawa, Ontario.

"Laura Secord" from *Legendary Heroes / Héros Légendaires* 1992. Courtesy of Canada Post Corporation, Ottawa, Ontario.

"Jerry Potts, Plainsman" from *Legendary Heroes / Héros Légendaires* 1992. Courtesy of Canada Post Corporation, Ottawa, Ontario.

"The Blue," "A Sudden Measure," "The Grass," and "Indian Summer" from *Rocky Mountain Foot* by George Bowering. Used by permission of the Canadian Publishers, McClelland & Stewart, Toronto.

"Chinook" from *Folktales / Contes Populaires* 1991. Courtesy of Canada Post Corporation, Ottawa, Ontario.

How Summer Came to Canada by William Toye, © Oxford University Press Canada, 1969. Reproduced by permission of the publisher. This retelling was freely based in part on the version in *Canadian Wonder Tales* by Cyrus Macmillan © The Bodley Head, Limited.

"Raven and the Whale" from *Raven Creator of the World* by Ronald Melzack. Reproduced by permission of the author.

Scenes from *The Magnificent Voyage of Emily Carr* © 1992 by Jovette Marchessault, English translation © 1992 by Linda Gaboriau, Talon Books Ltd., Vancouver, Canada.

The Fire Stealer retold by William Toye, © Oxford University Press Canada, 1979. Reproduced by permission of the publisher.

Roses Sing on New Snow. Text copyright © 1991 by Paul Yee, illustrations copyright © 1991 by Harvey Chan. A Groundwood Book/Douglas & McIntyre Ltd.

"A Poor Cottage" from "A Woman of the Foxes" in *Yellow-Wolf and Other Tales of the Saint Lawrence* by Philippe-Joseph Aubert de Gaspé, English translation © 1990 by Jane Brierly. Published by Véhicule Press, Montréal, Québec.

"River of My Eyes" by Saint-Denys Garneau. Reprinted from *Complete Poems of Saint-Denys Garneau*, translated by John Glassco. Used by permission of Oberon Press, Ottawa.

"North Stream" from *Selected Poems* by F. R. Scott. Used by permission of the Canadian Publishers, McClelland & Stewart, Toronto.

"Waiting for the First Drop" by Raymond Souster is reprinted from *Collected Poems of Raymond Souster* by permission of Oberon Press, Ottawa.

The Enchanted Caribou by Elizabeth Cleaver. Used by permission of the author's estate.

Chapter 6 of *Naomi's Road* by Joy Kogawa. Used by permission of the author.

"What Do I Remember of the Evacuation?" from *A Choice of Dreams* by Joy Kogawa. Used by permission of the Canadian Publishers, McClelland & Stewart, Toronto.

reface

Classics Canada: Authentic Readings for ESL Students is a reading series of authentic texts of Canadian literature for young adult and adult learners of English as a Second or a Foreign Language.

We have tried to reflect the many social, cultural, and linguistic groups that make up Canadian society. You will be exposed to the different ways Canadians write and speak so that, when you leave the classroom, you will be prepared to communicate with English speakers from all regions of Canada.

There are four levels in the series. In each level, there are two components:

- a student's book
- an audio cassette tape

We suggest that you keep a journal in a notebook or a looseleaf binder. In the journal, you can write your answers to all the warm-up and reading activities, keep track of new vocabulary words and expressions, and experiment with the topics in the discussion and writing activities. If you wish, you may also record your thoughts and impressions of the reading selections and the library books.

ORGANIZATION OF THE STUDENT'S BOOK

The student's book contains 15 chapters with a variety of texts and tasks. Each chapter follows this pattern:

- warm-up activities
- text
- glossary
- reading comprehension activity
- listening comprehension activity
- discussion and writing activities
- library books

Warm-Up

The Warm-Up consists of brief activities that are designed to acquaint you with the context of the selection and to interest you in reading it.

Text

Each student's book in *Classics Canada* consists of short stories, poems, scenes from plays, and chapters from novels, reprinted in their complete, unaltered forms.

Although a few minor corrections have been made for the sake of accuracy, the literary texts are reproduced as published. As a result, there are some variations among the texts in spelling, capitalization, punctuation, and the use of accent marks.

You will listen to the text on cassette and read it silently at the same time. You should not stop reading if you come across an unfamiliar word. Try to figure out the meaning of new words and expressions from the context.

Glossary

The glossary defines new words and expressions according to the context of the story. As you listen to and read the story silently a second time, you should refer to these definitions.

If time permits, you can read the story a third time and write any words or expressions that are still unfamiliar to you in a journal. You may look them up in a dictionary, ask another student, or ask the teacher for the definitions, and write them in the journal.

Reading Activity

The reading comprehension activities are intended to teach you, not test you. There are activities on reading for the main ideas, reading for details, understanding the meaning of words from the context, and inferring meaning from what is not stated directly.

Listening Activity

The listening comprehension activities are designed to provide you with short, interesting texts spoken in English. There are meaningful tasks such as aural cloze, short responses, dictation, and interactive dictation.

Discussion and Writing Activities

Several activities are suggested in each chapter. Some activities are more appropriate for oral work, others for written work. You could either choose one or more of these activities, or use an original idea of your own. It is best to vary these activities so that you do some on your own, others in pairs, and still others in small or large groups.

Library Books

The Library Books section lists reading material by the same author or on the same topic as the text. We strongly encourage you to read more on the topic outside of class time. That is, after all, the aim of the series.

We hope you enjoy reading the book as much as we have enjoyed writing it. We also hope you come to know and love Canada as much as we do. Please let us know what you think and how you feel about this book in the series. We look forward to meeting you again in Book 2 of *Classics Canada: Authentic Readings for ESL Students.*

CHAPTER ONE

The Loup-Garou
The Legend from Beauséjour, Quebec

Courtesy of Peter Nesbitt

WARM-UP

Look at the picture. How would you feel if you encountered such an animal, especially on a dark and lonely night?

Introduction to the Story

This is a legend, that is, a story told by people a long time ago. It is about two men, but one turns into a *loup-garou*, which is the French word for werewolf. According to some stories and legends, a werewolf is a person who sometimes becomes a wolf or a dog-like creature.

One man is a miller, a person who owns or works in a mill. The miller in this legend owns a flour mill, which is a building that contains a large machine for crushing corn or wheat or grain into flour. Try to explain in your own words what other kinds of mills do: pepper mills, coffee mills, paper mills, cotton mills, and windmills.

The second man becomes the miller's assistant and his friend. Then a frightening thing happens on Christmas Eve, the day before Christmas Day, which is on December 25th (or January 6th). Christmas Eve and Christmas Day are religious and public holidays in many places.

Think about these questions as you read the story: Who turns into a werewolf, the miller or his assistant? How and why does he become a werewolf? What happens at the mill on Christmas Eve? What happens to the miller and his assistant after that?

$\mathcal{T}$he Loup-Garou

You probably think werewolf stories are pretty far-fetched°. But there are still people in Québec who will tell you about their personal experiences with werewolves, or *loup-garous* as they are called. Many of them will also tell you what happened to Joachim Crête, the old miller from Beauséjour.

Poor old Crête. No one really liked him very much. For one thing, he snubbed° the villagers — except when they brought him grain to mill. For another, he broke the rules of the Church. He hadn't been to mass° or confession° in years, and on Sundays° almost always kept his mill turning.

One day, a stranger from the mountains named Hubert Sauvageau knocked on Crête's door looking for work. The man was rough and dirty in appearance and speech, and looked too young to do a good day's work°. However, Sauvageau promised to work hard for very little money. Best of all, he loved to play checkers° as much as Crête. The old man was delighted with his new assistant. The neighbours, however, were shocked by Sauvageau's foul language° and irreligious° ways and came to dislike him even more than they did Crête.

Soon everyone in the area began to spread terrifying rumours about a *loup-garou*. No one had actually seen the beast but there was evidence everywhere — a sheep with its throat torn out, and a child that had been mangled° to death. Crête and Sauvageau were the only ones who didn't live in constant fear of the *loup-garou*. In fact, they laughed at their neighbours for being so superstitious°. Though most of the villagers were afraid even to open their doors at night, young Sauvageau would often go out late after his drunken boss had fallen asleep, slumped over the checker board.

On Christmas Eve, everyone ventured outside to go to midnight mass — everyone, that is, except Crête and Sauvageau. Not only were the two men celebrating wildly, they were keeping the mill turning. After the church bells rang at midnight, however, their celebrations were interrupted.

Crête put down his glass and listened. "Did you hear that?" he asked.

"I don't hear a thing," said Sauvageau.

"That's what I mean — the mill just stopped dead!"

Swearing as they went, they descended into the millroom with a lantern. They tried to get the mill turning again but it wouldn't budge.

"The devil with it!°" Crête cursed. "Let's get out of here."

At that very moment, the lantern went out and left them in a silent darkness. As they groped° their way up the stairs, Sauvageau fell. Crête ignored him, however, and weaved° his way back to the kitchen.

Just then, he heard a groaning sound behind him. When he turned around, he almost died of fright. Standing there was a huge black dog with long fangs°, staring savagely at him.

"Help! Hubert!" he called out. There wasn't a sound except for the animal's panting°. "Hubert!"

Just as the beast was about to pounce°, the church bell rang again and Crête fell to his knees. "My God," he cried. "Please save me from the *loup-garou*!"

Fortunately, there was a sickle° within easy reach. He struck the *loup-garou* with it and fainted.

When Crête awoke the next day, Sauvageau was splashing water on his face. Before he could ask what had happened, he noticed a gash° on the young man's ear. In a flash, he realized that Sauvageau was the *loup-garou*.

"It was you!" he cried and fainted once again. The old miller apparently never regained his senses° after that and died some years later.

GLOSSARY

far-fetched (adj)	improbable or difficult to believe
snubbed (people) (v)	treated them rudely, paid no attention to them
mass (n)	an important religious service in many Christian religions

confession (n)	a religious practice in which a person tells his or her sins to a priest
on Sundays (exp)	according to the rules of the Christian Church, Sunday is the day when people do not work; they rest and relax
a good day's work (exp)	working hard for the whole day
checkers (n)	*checkers* in North American English; *draughts* in British English; a game played by two people, each with 12 round pieces on a checker board of 64 squares
foul language (n)	swear words or curses
irreligious (adj)	not obeying the rules of a religion very carefully
mangled (v)	torn or cut into pieces; crushed
superstitious (adj)	believing in things that are not based on reason or logic, but on magic and old ideas
The devil with it! (exp)	a swear or a curse that means send something to the devil or Satan, the most powerful evil spirit
groped (v)	searched about with the hands, in the dark or as if in the dark
weaved (v)	moved along, turning and changing direction frequently
fangs (n)	long, sharp teeth, such as those of a snake, a dog, or a wolf
panting (v)	taking quick, short breaths, especially after great effort or great heat
pounce (v)	fly down or spring suddenly in order to seize something
sickle (n)	a farm tool with a short handle and a curved blade used for cutting tall grass and weeds
gash (n)	a deep cut
regained his senses (exp)	became conscious; got his powers of thinking back

There may be other words and expressions in the story that are not familiar to you. Write each one in your journal. Then look it up in a dictionary, ask another student, or ask the teacher for a definition. Write the definition on the line beside the word or expression. Try to use the new word or expression in a sentence.

READING ACTIVITY

Inference Questions

Sometimes you can find information in a story that is not stated clearly in the words. You infer the information — that is, you make a logical guess — from either what is in the text, or your knowledge of the world, or both.

Try to infer the probable answers to the questions below by looking at the story. Be ready to give your reasons.

1. How did Crête and Sauvageau celebrate Christmas Eve?
2. Why did the mill suddenly stop turning?
3. Why did Crête's lantern go out?
4. Why did Sauvageau fall down the stairs?
5. Why did Crête ignore Sauvageau when he fell?
6. Why did Sauvageau ignore Crête when he called for help?
7. Why did Crête faint or lose consciousness?
8. Why was Sauvageau splashing water on his face the next morning?
9. How did Sauvageau get a gash on his ear?
10. Why did Crête faint again?

LISTENING ACTIVITY

Werewolves

How much do you know about werewolves? Try to guess the answers to these questions. Be ready to give your reasons.

1. What do werewolves do to people and animals?
2. Why do people tell legends about werewolves?
3. When did people begin to tell legends about werewolves?

4. How do people destroy werewolves?

5. What do werewolves look like?

6. Why does a person turn into a werewolf?

7. How does a werewolf become a person again?

First, listen to the text. Second, listen to the text and fill in the blanks in your journal. Third, listen to the text and correct and complete the blanks. Now discuss the answers to the questions about werewolves with the teacher and other students.

Werewolves are one of the most frightening of beasts — real or imagined — ever to roam the earth.

Not only do they viciously attack and kill their (1) _____, they are particularly fond of human flesh. And, as Joachim Crête (2) _____, a friend by day may turn out to be a (3) _____ by night.

There are many reasons why people the (4) _____ over have been taken for werewolves. One explanation is (5) _____; another is a rare disease that causes long hair (6) _____ grow over all parts of the body, including the (7) _____.

Regardless of the current theories, stories about werewolves date (8) _____ to Greek and Roman times.

By the Middle Ages, (9) _____ throughout civilized Europe lived in terror of the (10) _____. The French, for example, took werewolves so seriously that (11) _____ executed them! As recently as 1720, a werewolf discovered (12) _____ Austria was hanged, mutilated, and burned to prevent it (13) _____ coming back as a vampire.

According to French-Canadian (14) _____, a *loup-garou* may take the form of another animal (15) _____ as a dog or a bear. Whatever the animal, (16) _____ person becomes a *loup-garou* for failing to go to (17) _____ — especially at Easter Mass — for seven years.

The only (18) _____ this person can permanently return to human form is (19) _____ have someone strike the beast forcefully enough to draw (20) _____. Once delivered, the victim is left with a permanent scar, the only evidence of a murderous past.

DISCUSSION AND WRITING ACTIVITIES

My Favourite Board Game

Talk or write about your favourite board game with the teacher and other students. Which game do you like to play? Why? How is it played? How often do you play? Who wins?

Werewolf Stories

Talk or write about a werewolf story with the teacher and other students. Here is one way to begin your story.

You probably think werewolf stories are pretty far-fetched. But there are still people who will tell you about their personal experiences with werewolves. Many of them will also tell you what happened to...

The "Poor Old" Person

Talk or write about a story of a "poor old" person with the teacher and other students. Here is one way to begin your story.

Poor old X. No one really liked him / her very much. For one thing, he / she snubbed everyone. For another, he / she broke the rules that everyone else followed.

The Stranger at the Door

Create a legend of a stranger who comes knocking at your door. Talk or write about it with the teacher and other students. Here is one way to begin your story.

One day, a stranger knocked on the door looking for work. He / she looked too young to do a good day's work. However, he / she promised to work hard for very little money. Best of all, he / she loved to...

The Terrifying Rumour

Complete this story about a terrifying rumour. Talk or write about it with the teacher and other students.

Everyone in the area began to spread terrifying rumours. No one had actually seen anything, but there was evidence everywhere. The rumour was...

Complete this story about a blackout at midnight. Talk or write about it with the teacher and other students.

> *Everyone was having a good time at the party. At midnight, however, their celebrations were interrupted. The electricity went off.*
>
> *Some of them descended into the basement with a flashlight. They tried to get the power on again but there was a total blackout. At that very moment, the flashlight went out and left them in a silent darkness.*
>
> *As they groped their way up the stairs, they heard a groaning sound behind them. When they turned around, they almost died of fright. Standing there was...*

LIBRARY BOOKS

Do creatures such as werewolves really exist or are they pure fiction? And what about other monster-like creatures in Canada, such as Kraken from the ocean waters around Newfoundland, Ogopogo from Okanagan Lake in British Columbia, and Sasquatch or Bigfoot from the West Coast? You can read about them in the following books.

Legendary Creatures — Créatures Légendaires
(Ottawa: Canada Post, 1990)
Available at most post offices in Canada.

Werewolves
Jim Haskins
(New York: Watts, 1981)
Uses legends of different countries to discuss actual cases of werewolves, ways to protect oneself against these creatures, and how to cure an afflicted person.

If you would like to read about wolves, look for these books in the class, school, or local library, or in a bookstore.

Arctic Wolf
David L. Mech
(Toronto: Key Porter, 1985)
An introduction to the life of the Arctic wolf.

In Praise of Wolves
R. D. Lawrence
(Toronto: Key Porter, 1990)
Sympathetic account of the true nature of wolves covering hunting methods and social structures of packs. Another of Lawrence's books on the same subject is *Trail of the Wolf* (Toronto: Key Porter, 1993).

Never Cry Wolf
Farley Mowat
(Toronto: McClelland & Stewart, 1963)
A humorous and informative book arguing that wolves are not the vicious animals of legend, but are necessary and useful in the natural cycle.

With Ptarmigan and Tundra Wolves
Cy Hapson
(Victoria: Orca, 1991)
Discusses animal behaviour in Arctic regions.

Wolfman
L. P. Pringle
(New York: Scribner's, 1983)
A career biography of a wildlife biologist who spent 25 years studying the wolf.

CHAPTER TWO

Laura Secord

A Legendary Canadian Hero

Courtesy of Laura Secord Inc.

WARM-UP

Look at the picture carefully. This is Laura Ingersoll Secord. According to the clothes she is wearing, when and where do you think she lived?

Laura Ingersoll Secord became a famous Canadian patriot. What do you think she did to deserve that distinction?

Scanning

Read the questions below. The answer to each question can be found in the story about Laura Secord. Read the story quickly, looking for the information that will answer each question. You do not need to understand everything in the story. However, you must read carefully enough to find the answer to each question. This kind of reading to find information is called scanning. Try to answer each question in 30 seconds or less.

1. Who came to the Secord house?
2. What plan did he talk about?
3. Who heard about the plan?
4. Where and when did this happen?
5. What happened the year before that?
6. What did Laura decide to do?

Introduction to the Story

Think about these questions as you read the story: Why did the American soldiers talk openly about the plan? How did Laura feel about the Americans? How did she feel about the British? Why did the Indians (First Nations) help her? What happened to her after they helped her?

$\mathcal{L}$aura Secord

One warm summer evening in 1813, there was a loud knock at the door of Laura and James Secord's home, in the town of Queenston on the Niagara River. Ever since the Americans had declared war on the British a year earlier, Laura had been wary° about opening her door. Several months before, invading American troops had ransacked° the Secord home, stealing or destroying anything of value. To add to this hardship°, her husband James had been wounded in battle and still could not walk. The Americans now occupied the town and no one's home was safe. There was another knock, louder than the first. Laura sent her five children upstairs and went to open the door. Outside stood four American soldiers. They barged in°, sat at the dining table and demanded to be fed. Laura quickly laid out all the food she had prepared for supper, then quietly slipped out the back door. Sitting by an open window, she overheard one of the men boasting° to the others.

"FitzGibbon is finally going to get what he deserves!" he chortled°. "In two days, I'll be leading a surprise attack on his headquarters at Beaver Dams and capture every blasted one of his men. The entire Niagara Peninsula will be ours, and you'll have me, Cyrenius Chapin, to thank for it!"

Laura was stunned°. She knew that FitzGibbon was the British lieutenant who commanded a nearby outpost° and had recently captured several Americans, much to Chapin's annoyance. It now appeared that FitzGibbon and his men were in grave° danger.

Laura waited in the shadows until the soldiers had left, then ran upstairs to tell her bedridden° husband what she had learned.

"Someone has to warn FitzGibbon," said James, "but it can't be me..."

"I'll go!" Laura said, and despite her husband's objections, she made preparations to leave the next morning. Just before dawn, Laura departed without a sound. She first stopped in St. David's to see if her half-brother° Charles, who had been ill, was well enough to accompany her. Charles unfortunately was still not fit to move, but Laura's niece Elizabeth was eager to go with her.

The two women had to keep to° the woods to avoid being stopped by the American guards, though it meant a much longer and more difficult journey than the fifteen-kilometre route along the main road. Soon they were wading through swampland° and baking in the sweltering° heat. It all proved too much for Elizabeth. Weak and exhausted, she stayed behind with friends while Laura pressed on° alone.

Laura was soon following a creek that she knew flowed past FitzGibbon's outpost. Her blistered° feet pained her at every step. By nightfall, however, she had managed to cross over on a fallen tree almost within sight of the outpost when suddenly she was surrounded by a group of Indians. "Woman! Woman!" they began shouting, as startled° by her presence as she was by theirs. Frightened though Laura was, she managed to persuade the chief to take her to FitzGibbon.

Before long, she was standing barefoot° and bedraggled° before the famous lieutenant. He listened intently to her story, quite taken by° her remarkable courage.

"Madam, I believe that we owe you a great deal. Let me begin by offering you food and rest."

With that, the relieved but exhausted Laura fainted at the lieutenant's feet.

Two days later, when Laura was back safe at home, she learned it was the Americans who were taken by surprise at Beaver Dams, and all 462 men had surrendered to FitzGibbon.

GLOSSARY

wary (adj)	careful; looking out for danger
ransacked (v)	searched through and robbed
hardship (n)	difficult conditions of life, such as a lack of money or food
barged in (v)	rushed in rudely; interrupted
boasting (v)	saying or talking too proudly; expressing self-praise
chortled (v)	gave a laugh of pleasure or satisfaction; chuckled
stunned (adj)	shocked; very surprised
outpost (n)	a group of people or a settlement at some distance from the main group or settlement
grave (adj)	serious or solemn
bedridden (adj)	unable to get out of bed because of illness, injury or old age
half-brother (n)	a brother related through one parent only
keep to (v)	move or stay in a certain position
swampland (n)	an area of soft, wet land
sweltering (adj)	very hot
pressed on (v)	continued; advanced; went forward without delay
blistered (adj)	thin, watery swellings under the skin, caused by rubbing or burning
startled (adj)	suddenly surprised or frightened
barefoot (adj)	with no shoes or socks or other covering on the feet
bedraggled (adj)	with clothes and hair in disorder
taken by (v)	impressed by

There may be other words and expressions in the story that are not familiar to you. Write each one in your journal. Then look it up in a dictionary, ask another student, or ask the teacher for a definition. Write the definition on the line beside the word or expression. Try to use the new word or expression in a sentence.

READING ACTIVITY

True or False

You may want to look back and scan the text during this activity. When you scan, you read quickly to find certain bits of information. Beside each number in your journal, write **T** if the sentence is true according to the text, **F** if the sentence is false according to the text, and **DS** if the text doesn't say. Discuss the answers with the teacher and other students.

1. The Americans declared war on the British in 1812.
2. Laura's brother walked with her to St. David's.
3. Cyrenius Chapin was an American soldier.
4. James Secord was shot when the Americans ransacked the Secord home.
5. Lieutenant FitzGibbon's headquarters was at Beaver Dams.
6. The British soldiers helped Laura get back home.
7. Elizabeth was Laura's sister.
8. The Indians (First Nations) thought Laura was an American.

LISTENING ACTIVITY

Laura Ingersoll Secord

This is a summary of important dates in the life of Laura Ingersoll Secord. First, listen to the text. Second, listen to the text and fill in the blanks in your journal. Third, listen to the text and complete the blanks. Discuss the answers with the teacher and other students.

1775	Laura Ingersoll was born in Massachusetts Colony.
1783	_____
1795	Laura's father took the family to the Niagara Peninsula in Upper Canada.
1797	_____
_____	The Americans declared war on Britain and Canada.
1813	_____
_____	Laura lived in poverty with her invalid husband and seven children.
1841	_____
_____	The public learned of Laura's role in the victory against the Americans.
1860	_____

DISCUSSION AND WRITING ACTIVITIES

Laura Ingersoll Secord: Canadian Hero

Use the information in the Listening Activity above to write a summary of the life of Laura Ingersoll Secord.

War of 1812 Heroes

The people mentioned below were also involved in the War of 1812. Choose one name and find out some information about this person and the times in which he lived. Then talk or write about your information with other students.

General Isaac Brock
John Richardson
Lieutenant-Colonel Charles-Michel de Salaberry
Tecumseh
William "Tiger" Dunlop

War of 1812 Battles

The battles mentioned below were important in the War of 1812. Choose one of them and find out some information about the battle and the people who were involved in it. Then talk or write about your information with other students.

Battle of Châteauguay
Queenston Heights
The Capture of Detroit

Heroes

Think about a person or a group of people who performed a heroic act for a cause that the individual or the group believed in. Talk or write about that person or group with the teacher and other students.

Chocolate Candy

The name of Laura Secord is used by the Laura Secord Candy Company today. It is famous for the chocolate candy that it makes and sells throughout Canada. Talk or write about chocolates and chocolate candy with the teacher and other students.

Laura Secord Inc.

Write a letter to one of these organizations: Laura Secord Inc. or Nestlé Canada Inc. Ask the organization for information about (1) the history of Laura Ingersoll Secord, (2) the restoration of the Laura Secord Homestead, and (3) the history of the Laura Secord Candy Company. When you receive the information, read it carefully. Did you learn any other facts about Laura Secord? What are they?

LIBRARY BOOKS

If you enjoyed reading about the War of 1812 patriot Laura Secord, you may wish to read about the adventures of other Canadian heroes from the 19th century: Jos Montferrand, legendary lumberjack, and Captain William Jackman, sea rescuer. In the following book, you can read some fascinating facts about the lives of these remarkable people who showed courage and bravery in the face of danger.

Legendary Heroes — Héros Légendaires
(Ottawa: Canada Post, 1992)
Available at most post offices in Canada.

If you would like to read more about Laura Secord herself, look for these books in the class, school, or local library, or in a bookstore.

Laura Secord
John Bassett
(Toronto: Fitzhenry & Whiteside, 1974)
An illustrated book for young adults.

Laura Secord
Ruth McKenzie
(Toronto: McClelland & Stewart, 1971)
An illustrated biography of Laura Secord.

If you would like to read more about the times in which Laura Secord lived, look for these books in the class, school, or local library, or in a bookstore.

At Home in Upper Canada
Jeanne Minhinnick
(Toronto: Clarke, Irwin, 1970)
An illustrated look at the life of the early settlers.

The Capture of Detroit
Pierre Berton
(Toronto: McClelland & Stewart, 1993)
The story of the first Canadian victory of the War of 1812. Several famous Canadians took part in this surprise victory, including General Isaac Brock, Shawnee war chief Tecumseh, and novelist John Richardson.

The Death of Isaac Brock
Pierre Berton
(Toronto: McClelland & Stewart, 1993)
An illustrated look at the battle of Queenston Heights, in which a small force of regular soldiers, Mohawks, and settlers defeated a much larger American army. The most important battle of the war.

1812
John Ibbotson
(Toronto: Macmillan, 1991)
A novel for young adults about a boy's adventures during the War of 1812.

The Invasion of Canada, 1812-1813
Pierre Berton
(Toronto: McClelland & Stewart, 1980)
The first volume of a popular history of the War of 1812. The second and final volume is *Flames Across the Border, 1813-1814* (Toronto: McClelland & Stewart, 1981).

Life in Upper Canada
Wesley B. Turner
(Toronto: Grolier, 1980)
An illustrated history of Upper Canada until 1841.

Redcoat
Gregory Sass
(Erin, Ontario: Porcupine's Quill, 1985)
A novel about a boy who runs away from home and enlists in General Brock's regiment.

The War of 1812
Wesley B. Turner
(Toronto: Grolier, 1982)
An illustrated look at the issues and events surrounding the war.

CHAPTER THREE

Jerry Potts, Plainsman

A Legendary Canadian Hero

Courtesy of R.C.M.P. Museum, Regina, Sask.

WARM-UP

Look at the picture carefully. This is Jerry Potts. He was born of an aboriginal mother and a Scottish father so he was a Métis, a member of a group of people in western Canada who are half aboriginal and half European. He is a legendary Canadian hero. What do you think he did to deserve that distinction?

Skimming

Sometimes we want to have a general idea about a piece of writing before we read it carefully. This activity will show you one way of doing that.

Take one minute (60 seconds) to read the first two sentences of each paragraph in the story. This kind of fast reading for the general idea is called skimming. Next, try to answer the following questions. Do not look back at the story to answer them.

1. When did the North West Mounted Police first meet Jerry Potts?
2. Who hired Jerry Potts to work for the North West Mounted Police?
3. Why did the North West Mounted Police come to southern Alberta?
4. What was Jerry Potts's first assignment for the North West Mounted Police?
5. What other jobs did Jerry Potts do for the North West Mounted Police?

Introduction to the Story

Think about these questions as you read the story: Why were the North West Mounted Police organized? How did they establish law and order in the West? How did Jerry Potts feel about the Americans? about the First Nations (aboriginal) peoples? about the Mounties?

Jerry Potts, Plainsman°

(1)   In September 1874, when the newly formed North West Mounted Police° hired Métis scout Jerry Potts, they were desperate indeed. Abandoned by their own guides after a 1500-kilometre trek° from Manitoba across the hot dusty plains to Sweetgrass Hills in southwest Alberta, the 300 Mounties were starving° and near exhaustion.

(2)   Colonel George French, who was in command, and his assistant Colonel James Macleod, had headed° south into Montana to Fort Benton to pick up supplies and hire a guide familiar with the area. Everyone at the trading post° had said that Potts, who spoke many Indian languages, was the best guide around. When Potts shambled° in, however, the rather stern° Colonel French had his doubts. Small and bowlegged°, Potts had a wide moustache and narrow shoulders. He wore the bowler hat°, jacket and trousers of a white man, and the leggings, moccasins° and knife belt of an Indian. Knowing that he could not afford to be fussy°, however, French held out his hand.

(3)   "How do you do, Mr. Potts?" said the colonel and hired him on the spot.

(4)   On the way back to Sweetgrass Hills, French explained to Potts that the Mounted Police had come to establish law and order in the west. Potts knew only too well about the Americans and their illegal liquor trade across the

Canadian frontier. Worst of all, whisky was destroying the Blackfoot Indians°, who were giving up everything or killing each other off to get it. "It seems that the only law out here," said French, "is the kind men carry in their holsters°."

(5)   Macleod's first assignment was to capture the notorious whisky trading post, Fort Whoop-Up°, in southern Alberta. Macleod took command of half the force and set out one morning with Potts as their guide. With the instincts of a homing pigeon°, Potts rode across the treeless hills well ahead of the troops. By evening, he was waiting for them at a grassy campsite with plenty of spring water and buffalo meat ready for supper.

(6)   For days, Potts led the weary caravan° over seemingly endless terrain, riding alone and seldom speaking a word. When they arrived at Fort Whoop-Up, Macleod and Potts rode through the gates only to find one old man inside. The whisky traders had fled the country and the Mounties were able to take over the fort without firing a single shot.

(7)   Potts' next task was to find a suitable site on which to build an outpost. He guided the soldiers to a 250-hectare island in the Oldman River, with plenty of trees for wood and grass to graze the horses. While the future Fort Macleod was being built, Potts visited neighbouring tribes of Blackfoot, who were suspicious of the red-coated° strangers. By explaining why they had come, he was able to persuade his Indian brothers not to attack. Later, he invited three tribal chiefs to the fort to meet Macleod. Hands were shaken, a peace pipe° was smoked and, by turns, the three chiefs spoke at length to Macleod. When they finally finished speaking, Macleod anxiously awaited Potts' translation.

(8)   "What did they say?" Macleod asked.

(9)   Potts shrugged his shoulders and said, "They damn glad you're here." Potts may not have been the best interpreter, but without him the Mountie force would not have survived that first winter. On one expedition, he guided Macleod and several others through a howling blizzard° despite the fact that he was snow blind° the last several kilometres. In six short months, Potts had become invaluable to the police force. He would stay loyal to them for 22 years until his death.

GLOSSARY

plainsman (n)	a person who lives on the plains
North West Mounted Police (n)	the original name of the Royal Canadian Mounted Police, the federal police force of Canada; in all provinces except Quebec and Ontario, the RCMP also act as provincial police; the NWMP and the RCMP are called the "Mounties"

trek (n)	a long, hard journey, especially on foot
starving (adj)	dying or suffering from lack of food
headed (v)	moved in a certain direction
trading post (n)	a place where people buy, sell, or exchange goods
shambled (v)	walked awkwardly, dragging the feet
stern (adj)	showing firmness towards the behaviour of others
bowlegged (adj)	having the legs curve outward at the knee
bowler hat (n)	a round hard hat, usually black
moccasins (n)	shoes made of soft leather
fussy (adj)	too much concerned about small matters and details
Blackfoot Indians (n)	the name of a First Nations group in the western part of North America
holsters (n)	leather holders for pistols (small handguns), especially ones that hang on a belt around the waist
Fort Whoop-Up (n)	a name given to a particular fort in which the people "whoop it up" or behave in a wild and crazy manner
homing pigeon (n)	a quite large short-legged bird that is able to fly to a particular destination to deliver a message and then flies back to its home
caravan (n)	a group of people with animals or vehicles travelling together for protection, especially through unfriendly areas
red-coated (adj)	wearing a red coat; the Mounties are famous for the bright red coats they wear as part of their uniforms
peace pipe (n)	a pipe filled with tobacco that First Nations peoples smoked with strangers as a sign of peace and friendship
blizzard (n)	a long, severe snowstorm
snow blind (adj)	unable to see because of the snow

There may be other words and expressions in the story that are not familiar to you. Write each one in your journal. Then look it up in a dictionary, ask another student, or ask the teacher for a definition. Write the definition on the line beside the word or expression. Try to use the new word or expression in a sentence.

READING ACTIVITY

Paragraph Names

You may want to look back and skim the text while doing this activity. When you skim, you read quickly to get the general idea of the text. From the list below, choose the best title for each paragraph in the story. In your journal, write the title letter next to the paragraph number. Be careful. There are only seven titles in all, so two paragraphs will not have titles. Discuss the answers with the teacher and other students.

Paragraph 1   a) Loyal to the End

Paragraph 2   b) The Goal of the Mounted Police

Paragraph 3   c) Arrival at Fort Whoop-Up

Paragraph 4   d) Abandoned in Alberta

Paragraph 5   e) Building Fort Macleod

Paragraph 6   f) A Guide Is Hired

Paragraph 7   g) Setting Out for Fort Whoop-Up

Paragraph 8

Paragraph 9

LISTENING ACTIVITY

Jerry Potts

This is a summary of the life of Jerry Potts. First, listen to the text. Second, listen to the text and complete each statement below by choosing the best response. Third, listen to the text and check your responses. Discuss the answers with the teacher and other students.

1. Jerry Potts was born in 1840
   a) in India.
   b) in Scotland.
   c) in Montana.

2. Andrew Dawson was the man who
   a) murdered the father of Jerry Potts.
   b) adopted Jerry Potts as a baby.
   c) took good care of Jerry Potts as a boy.

3. Jerry Potts's mother taught him how to
   a) speak several Indian (First Nations) languages.
   b) live in the Blood Indian culture.
   c) hunt, trap, and track game.

4. Jerry Potts was able to find a way to get to unknown places
   a) by using a map or a compass.
   b) by looking at the stars in the sky.
   c) by relying on his extraordinary talent.

5. Jerry Potts became famous as a great fighter because
   a) he scalped 16 people in one battle.
   b) he was wounded in battle only once.
   c) he possessed supernatural powers.

6. When Jerry Potts and his best friend used to drink,
   a) they would gamble and fight with each other.
   b) they would shoot at each other's moustaches.
   c) they would trade whisky with other people.

7. Jerry Potts worked with the Mounties because he wanted to
   a) bring peace back to his people.
   b) become a guide and a diplomat.
   c) shape the history of the West.

DISCUSSION AND WRITING ACTIVITIES

Translation

Jerry Potts had his own way of translating from one language to another. For example, he often reduced long speeches to a few short words: "He says he's damned glad to see you." Talk or write about an experience that you have had or that you have heard of which concerns the translation of something into another language. Be specific and provide concrete details about the incident so that your listeners or readers know exactly what happened.

People in Western Canada

Like Jerry Potts, the people mentioned below were also involved in the history of western Canada. Choose one name and find out some information about this person and the times in which he lived. Then talk or write about your information with other students.

Chief Crowfoot
Cuthbert Grant
Gabriel Dumont
George Arthur French
James Farquharson Macleod
Louis Riel

Places in Western Canada

The places mentioned below were also important in the history of western Canada. Choose one of them and find out some information about this place and the people who were associated with it. Then talk or write about your information with other students.

Fort Mackenzie
Fort Macleod
Fort Benton
Fort Saskatchewan
Fort Calgary
Fort Walsh

Events in Western Canada

The activities and events mentioned below were significant in the history of western Canada. Choose one of them and find out some information about the activities and events. Then talk or write about your information with other students.

Bison hunt
Fur trade
North-West Rebellion
Battle of Grand Coteau
Red River Rebellion
Métis Betterment Act

Plains First Nations

The aboriginal peoples are the original inhabitants of Canada. They are thus called the First Nations, and they lived in every region of Canada. Each group adapted to the land or sea in its own way. Each was affected by its neighbours and was constantly changing.

Despite the diversity of the First Nations, they are still referred to in three broad categories: the Inuit, the Indians, and the Métis. The Inuit are First Nations people who live in the Arctic. The Indians are First Nations people who are members of Indian bands. The Métis are people of mixed aboriginal and European ancestry. For example, Jerry Potts was part Plains Indian and part Scottish.

Choose one of these groups of Plains First Nations: (1) Assiniboine, (2) Blackfoot, (3) Gros Ventre, (4) Plains Cree, (5) Plains Métis, (6) Sarcee, or (7) Saulteaux.

Find out some information about the group, such as its history, territory, language, food, shelter, clothing, transportation, social and political organization, religion, art and leisure, or contemporary life.

Talk or write about the First Nations people that you have researched. In your opinion, what is the most interesting aspect of their culture?

The RCMP

Write a letter to either the local branch of the RCMP or to the RCMP in Ottawa, Ontario. Ask the organization for information about the origins of the Royal Canadian Mounted Police, the history of Jerry Potts, and the "Force" in the Yukon. When you receive the information, read it carefully. Did you learn any other facts about the RCMP or Jerry Potts? What are they?

LIBRARY BOOKS

If you would like to read more about Jerry Potts, look for these books in the class, school, or local library, or in a bookstore.

Jerry Potts
D. Bruce Sealey
(Toronto: Fitzhenry & Whiteside, 1980)
A short, illustrated biography.

Jerry Potts, Plainsman
Hugh A. Dempsey
(Calgary: Glenbow-Alberta Institute, 1984)
An illustrated biography.

If you would like to read more about the Métis people or the Mounties, look for these books in the class, school, or local library, or in a bookstore.

Hold High Your Heads
A. H. De Tremaudan
(Winnipeg: Pemmican, 1982)
A comprehensive history of the Métis people written from the Métis perspective. First published in French in 1935. Translated by Elizabeth Maguet.

Métis
D. Bruce Sealey
(Winnipeg: Pemmican, 1975)
A history of the Métis people with special emphasis on the current hardships that they face. Illustrated by Réal Bérard.

Riel's People
Maria Campbell
(Vancouver: Douglas & McIntyre, 1983)
An illustrated history of the Métis.

Soldier Boys
David Richards
(Winnipeg: Thistledown, 1993)
An adventure story about two Métis teenagers who become involved in the Riel Rebellion.

Best Mounted Police Stories
Dick Harrison, editor
(Edmonton: University of Alberta, 1983)
A collection of short stories about the Royal Canadian Mounted Police.

CHAPTER FOUR

Nature Poetry
GEORGE BOWERING

Al Harvey/The Slide Farm

WARM-UP

The poems in this chapter are written by a well-known Canadian author, George Bowering. He is not only a poet, but also a fiction writer, an editor, a critic, and a teacher. He has published over 40 books of poetry, fiction, and criticism.

Introduction to the Poems

Think about these questions as you read the poems: Who is the speaker in each poem? What kind of person does he or she seem to be? To whom is he or she speaking? What is the speaker's point of view and relation to the subject? What is the general mood or feeling (tone) of each poem? Is the feeling consistent from poem to poem or is there a shift in tone? What is the situation or occasion of each poem? What is the setting in time and space of each poem?

The four poems are about nature. If you wrote a poem about nature, what would you write about: the earth? the wind? the rain? the sky? the sun? the moon? the stars? Why? Listen to the poems and read them as many times as you wish.

 **oems**

Poem 1

The Bow River
was blue today,
the sky,
the Rockies somewhere

that is, the mud
has sunk,
the ice
disappeared sometime.

I would do that,
disappear sometime
like a blue river
on the prairie.

Poem 2

This sudden snow:
    immediately
the prairie is!

Those houses are:
    dark
under roofs of snow —

That hill up to the cloud is:
    marked
by snow creeks down to town —

This footpath is:
    a bare line
across white field —

    This woman appears
    thru° drift of snow:
a red coat.

Poem 3

I must tell you
of the brown grass
that has twenty times
this year, appeared
from under the
melting snow, reared
its version of spring
like a sea lion° coming
out of water, a-dazzle°
in the sun, this
brave grass the sun
will only burn again
returning like a tiny
season.

Poem 4

The yellow trees
along the river

are dying I said
they are in
their moment of life
you said.

The Indians I think
are dead, you can't
immortalize them, a

leaf presst° between
pages becomes a
page.

In a month
the river will move

beneath ice, moving
as it always does
south. We will
believe it as we

will no longer see
those yellow borders
of the river.

GLOSSARY

thru (prep)   through

sea lion (n)   large fish-eating sea animal with broad flat limbs
                           suitable for swimming; found in the Pacific Ocean

a-dazzle (adj)   a poetic version of "dazzling"; to make unable to see by
                           throwing a strong light in the eyes

presst (v)   a poetic spelling of the verb "pressed"; to direct weight
                           or force on something in order to crush, flatten, or pack
                           tightly

There may be other words and expressions in the poems that are not familiar to you. Write each one in your journal. Then look it up in a dictionary, ask another student, or ask the teacher for a definition. Write the definition on the line beside the word or expression. Try to use the new word or expression in a sentence.

READING ACTIVITIES

Mix and Match

Read the four poems again. Decide on an appropriate title for each poem and write it in your journal. Discuss your choices and the reasons for them with the teacher and other students.

Read the poems again and match them in your journal with the titles that George Bowering gave to them. Discuss your choices and the reasons for them with the teacher and other students.

Poem 1   a) "A Sudden Measure"
Poem 2   b) "Indian Summer"
Poem 3   c) "The Blue"
Poem 4   d) "The Grass"

A Poem Is...

Read the poems again and discuss the statements below with the teacher and other students. Be ready to give your reasons.

1. A poem always makes you think about words and their arrangement.
2. The lines of a poem always rhyme (that is, the lines end in words that sound almost the same).
3. A poem is always metrical (that is, there is a rhythm or a beat to the sound).
4. A poem is always about beauty.
5. A poem is always high-toned and moral.
6. A poem is always serious.

LISTENING ACTIVITY

George Bowering

This is a text on the life of George Bowering. First, listen to the text. Second, listen to the text and write as much of it as you can in your journal. Third, listen to the text and complete it. Then go over it with the teacher and the other students.

DISCUSSION AND WRITING ACTIVITIES

Identify the Types of Poetry

There are different types of poetry. Some of these types are ballads, lyrics, odes, and sonnets. Talk or write about the type of poems written by George Bowering. Are they all the same type, or are they different types? What is your favourite type of poetry? Why? Give a specific example.

Identify the Functions of Poetry

Poetry has different functions as well. Some poems narrate a story, others describe people, places, and things, and still others reflect upon thoughts and feelings. Talk or write about the function of the poems written by George Bowering. Do they all have the same function, or do they have different functions? What kind of poetry do you prefer: poetry that narrates, describes, or reflects? Why? Give a specific example.

Describe the Symbols and Images

Poetry often contains symbols, images, and figures of speech. If you are not sure what these terms mean, discuss them with the teacher and other students. Then talk or write about the symbols, images, and figures of speech in the poems written by George Bowering. Are they the same in all the poems, or are they different? Which symbol, image, or figure of speech in these poems do you admire the most? Why?

Describe the Rhyme and Metre

Poetry relies heavily on the sound and rhythm of speech, and often uses both rhyme and metre. If you are not sure what these terms mean, discuss them with the teacher and other students. Then talk or write about the rhyme and metre in the poems written by George Bowering. Are they the same in all the poems, or are they different? What is your favourite type of rhyme and metre in poetry? Why? Give a specific example

Evaluate the Poems by George Bowering

Talk or write about your evaluation of the poems. What is your reaction to each one? Do you like each one? If so, why? If not, why not? How do the poems compare to your own favourite poems? Why? Give a specific example.

Evaluate the Poet

Talk or write about your evaluation of George Bowering. Do you like his work? If so, why? If not, why not? How does George Bowering's work compare to the work of your own favourite poet?

LIBRARY BOOKS

If you would like to read other works by George Bowering, look for these books in the class, school, or local library, or in a bookstore.

Burning Water
(Toronto: New Press, 1983)
A novel about the 18th-century explorer, George Vancouver. Written for adults, this book won the 1980 Governor General's award for fiction.

George Bowering Selected Poems 1961-1992
(Toronto: McClelland & Stewart, 1993)
A large collection of some of Bowering's finest poetry. Edited by Roy Miki.

Mask in Place
(Winnipeg: Turnstone, 1982)
A collection of short essays on Canadian and American literature.

Rocky Mountain Foot
(Toronto: McClelland & Stewart, 1968)
A collection of poetry which, with *The Gangs of Kosmos* (Toronto: McClelland & Stewart, 1969), won Bowering the 1969 Governor General's Award for poetry.

If you would like to read about George Bowering, look for these books in the class, school, or local library, or in a bookstore.

George Bowering
Eva-Marie Kroller
(Vancouver: Talonbooks, 1992)
A critical look at the work of the poet.

George Bowering and His Works
John Harris
(Toronto: ECW, 1991)
A brief book combining biography and criticism.

A Record of Writing
Roy Miki
(Vancouver: Talonbooks, 1990)
An annotated and illustrated bibliography of the poet.

CHAPTER FIVE

The Chinook

A Canadian Tall Tale

© Patrick Morrow

WARM-UP

Look at the picture of the Rocky Mountains. Do you know where they are? Do you know where they begin and end? Do you know how high they are? Have you ever seen them? Have you ever taken a picture of them? Have you ever travelled across or through them? Tell the class about it.

This story is about a west wind that blows from the Pacific Ocean across the Rocky Mountains. It is cool and wet as it goes up one side of the Rockies, but it becomes warm and dry as it goes down the other side. This wind is called the chinook.

Scanning

Read the questions below. The answer to each question can be found in the story. Read the story quickly, looking for the information that will answer each question. You do not need to understand everything in the story, but you must read carefully enough to find the answer to each question. This kind of reading to find information is called scanning. Try to answer each question in 30 seconds or less.

1. In what year does the story take place?
2. Who and what is a greenhorn?
3. Who and what are the old timers?
4. What season of the year is it?
5. Where is the nearest city?
6. What kind of stories are the old timers telling Tom?
7. What are the stories about?
8. How many stories do they tell him?

Introduction to the Story

Think about these questions as you read the story: Why do the old timers tell the greenhorn these stories? How do you know that these stories are not true? What is your reaction to these tall tales?

The Chinook

To most of you, a chinook is just a warm, dry wind that blows out of the Rockies, but to pioneers° like Jack and Charlie Henderson, it was an extraordinary event. Back in 1890, a young eastern visitor or "greenhorn" named Tom found out from these old timers just what a chinook could do.

Tom had arrived late in the summer and found work on the Henderson's cattle ranch near the town of Calgary. One evening, after the branding° had been done, Tom was sitting in the house with the Henderson brothers and a couple of ranch hands°. No one would ever think that Jack and Charlie were brothers. Jack was lanky° and soft-spoken, while Charlie was built like a bull and always boisterous°.

The nights were already starting to get cool. Charlie stoked° the fire, then sat in his overstuffed° chair and lit his pipe. Since Tom had never spent a winter there, he asked Charlie if chinook winds were really as warm as people said. The old timer's eyes twinkled° as he puffed on his pipe.

"I'll tell you what happened to me a few winters back," he said, "and then you tell me if they're as warm as folks say they are. Fair enough?" Tom nodded. "We lived in Morley then, about 40 miles west of here. There must've been two feet of snow on the ground when I left for Calgary with the team and bobsleigh°. After a while, I heard a whistlin' at my back and I knew there was a chinook followin' me. So I whipped up the horses to a gallop° so as I'd reach town before the snow melted. Sure enough, the snow melted so darn fast that the front runners° were in the snow, but the back runners were draggin' in the mud! Isn't that right, Jack?" Tom stared at one, then the other.

"Yes, indeed," his brother replied, stroking his beard. "Reminds me of the time I was driving in from Morley with my wife in the back of the wagon. A chinook was chasing us, so I drove like blazes° and managed to stay ahead of it. Because by the time we got to Calgary, I had frostbite° and my wife had sunstroke°!" Tom did not know whether to laugh or not. Nobody else was.

"That's nothin'," said Fred, one of the ranch hands. "One winter, before you fellers° came out here, there was so much snow that every building in Calgary was covered by drifts°. I went to get provisions one day and the whole town had disappeared! So I turned 'round and headed west. But then a scorcher° of a chinook blew out of the mountains and I ended up havin' to swim back home!"

"Does it get very cold?" Tom asked.

"Cold?" Jack said, leaning forward in his rocking chair. "Well, years ago, when greenhorns like yourself came to Calgary, they didn't realize how cold it could get, so they never covered their ears. What a mistake that was. Lots of them had their ears frozen right off! And since they didn't want to go around with no ears, they got the local blacksmith° to make them artificial ones. First he tried making them out of leather but that didn't work so well. For one thing, they got all soft and floppy; for another, you'd get nuzzled° by horses all the time. Then he thought of making them out of tin. Them tin ears were a big success — except in a hailstorm°. Boy, the noise was deafening!"

"Probably makes more sense to wear a warm hat," said Charlie. "Or to wait for a chinook. Warms your ears up in no time." The old rancher's eyes were really twinkling now. "Like in the winter of '86. We were drivin' up to Edmonton — or tryin' to anyway — and had to camp for the night. So we tied the horses to some evergreens° and pitched our tent. We were so damn cold we just went straight to bed. When we woke up in the morning, we were in a sweat 'cause a chinook had come in the night. Then we went outside and realized that our horses were gone. We were lookin' everywhere for them and suddenly heard this strange sound up in the trees. We looked up and there were the horses — danglin' from the treetops!" Charlie leaned back and blew a stack of smoke rings that sailed right over Tom's head.

GLOSSARY

pioneers (n)	people who have settled in a region that is still mostly wilderness
branding (n)	a mark made (as by burning), usually to show ownership
ranch hands (n)	people, in particular cowboys, who work on a large farm, especially one where sheep, cattle, or horses are produced in the western part of Canada and the United States
lanky (adj)	(especially of a person) very thin and ungracefully tall
boisterous (adj)	(of a person or his/her behaviour) noisily cheerful and rough
stoked (v)	filled (an enclosed fire) with material (fuel) which is burned to give heat or power
overstuffed (adj)	too much padding stuffed under the material of upholstered furniture
twinkled (v)	were bright with amusement or delight
bobsleigh (n)	also *bobsled*; a small vehicle that runs on metal blades and is used for travelling over snow or sliding down snowy slopes
gallop (n)	the movement of a horse at its fastest speed
runners (n)	the two thin blades on which a sled or a sleigh slides over the snow
drove like blazes (exp)	drove as quickly and as recklessly as possible
frostbite (n)	swelling and discolouration of a person's limbs, caused by a great cold
sunstroke (n)	an illness caused by the effects of too much strong sunlight
fellers (n)	informal term for fellows, men, or guys

drifts (n)	a mass of matter (such as snow or sand) blown together by the wind
scorcher (n)	a very hot one
blacksmith (n)	a person who makes and repairs things made of iron, especially horseshoes, usually made by hand
nuzzled (v)	(especially of an animal) to rub, touch, or push with the nose
hailstorm (n)	a storm in which frozen raindrops fall very heavily as little hard balls
evergreens (n)	a tree or bush, such as pine or spruce, that does not lose its leaves or its needles in cold weather

There may be other words and expressions in the story that are not familiar to you. Write each one in your journal. Then look it up in a dictionary, ask another student, or ask the teacher for a definition. Write the definition on the line beside the word or expression. Try to use the new word or expression in a sentence.

READING ACTIVITIES

Standard English

Sometimes when people speak and write English, they do not use standard English. For example, Charlie Henderson says: "After a while, I heard a *whistlin'* at my back and I knew there was a chinook *followin'* me." In standard English, the words should be spelled *whistling* and *following*. Find at least five other examples of non-standard English and rewrite them in standard English.

Guess the Meaning of Words from Context

Scan the text and find words or phrases in it that seem to correspond to the definitions given below. Discuss the answers with the teacher and other students.

1. pile
2. fake
3. hanging
4. loud

5. big and soft
6. whiskers
7. set up
8. limp

Express Your Opinion

Discuss the answers to these questions with the teacher and other students:

1. Why do old timers tell greenhorns tall tales?
2. How do you know that these tall tales are not true?
3. What is your reaction to these tall tales?

LISTENING ACTIVITY

The Chinook

This is a text of amazing but true facts about the chinook. First, listen to the text. Second, listen to the text and answer each question below in your journal. Third, listen to the text and check your answers. Discuss the answers with the teacher and other students.

1. By how much can a chinook raise the air temperature?
2. How fast can chinook winds blow per hour?
3. When a chinook visits southern Alberta, what summer sport can be played?
4. According to Indian legend, what is the chinook and where does it come from?
5. According to weather specialists, what is the chinook and where does it come from?
6. What effect can a chinook have on cattle and farmers?
7. What effect can a chinook have on fruit trees?
8. What effect can a chinook have on the topsoil?

DISCUSSION AND WRITING ACTIVITIES

Retell a Tall Tale

Imagine that you are Tom or a greenhorn in 1890 in Calgary. Choose one of the five tall tales from "The Chinook" and retell it either orally or in writing in your own words.

- Charlie's tall tale about his horses and bobsleigh
- Jack's tall tale about his wife and wagon

- Fred's tall tale about his trip to Calgary
- Jack's tall tale about the blacksmith and the ears
- Charlie's tall tale about his trip to Edmonton

Tell a Tall Tale

Have you ever heard or read a tall tale? Talk or write about it with the teacher and other students. Then decide who has heard or read the most interesting tall tale.

Create a Tall Tale

Create and develop your own tall tale or wildly exaggerated story. Share it with the teacher and other students. Then decide who has told or written the best tall tale.

Weather Watch

Chinook-type winds occur in other parts of the world where there are geographical features similar to those in western Canada: mountains at right angles to the prevailing winds, which carry warm, moist air from an ocean. Here are some examples:

- the *foehn* of Austria and Switzerland
- the *hamsin* of Israel
- the Santa Ana wind of southern California
- the mistral wind of France
- the *sirocco* of the Mediterranean

These are warm, dry, and gusty westerly winds. Such winds seem to cause abnormal behaviour. Some people report feeling aggressive or listless just before these winds blow. Rates of accidents, crimes, and suicides increase.

Choose one of the famous winds listed above. Find out some information about it and its effect on people. Talk or write about this wind with the teacher and other students.

Unusual Weather

Have you experienced or do you know anyone who has experienced unusual weather, such as those mentioned below? If so, talk or write about it. If not, find out some information about one of them and share it with the rest of the class.

hail	flood
avalanche	hurricane
blizzard	tidal wave
drought	tornado
earthquake	volcanic eruption

The Weather and Climate in Canada

Write a letter to one of these government organizations: Environment Canada or Health and Welfare Canada. Ask the organization for general information about the weather and the climate in Canada, or request one of the following booklets or brochures:

"The Atmosphere: Out of Sight, Out of Mind?"
"The Climate: What a Difference a Degree Makes!"
"Explore Water"
"From the Mountains to the Sea"
"The Green Scene"
"Ozone: Guarding Our Earth"
"The Ozone Layer: What's Going On Up There?"
"Smog: Let's Clear the Air!"

When you receive the information, read it carefully. Did you learn any other facts about the weather and climate in Canada? What are they?

LIBRARY BOOKS

As well as tall tales about the warm chinook wind, there are other popular Canadian folktales. For example, there is the story about four fishermen who searched for mysterious pirate treasure one night on Oak Island in Nova Scotia. There is also a legend that in the winter lumber camps or "shanties" of Quebec, years ago, loggers could sail over miles of snow-covered terrain in a *chasse-galerie* or witch canoe, simply by making a deal with the devil. And there is a chilling Inuit legend from the eastern Arctic about Kaujakjuk, the orphan boy, who was so mistreated that he decided to seek revenge. You can read about them in the following books.

Folktales — Contes Populaires
(Ottawa: Canada Post, 1991)
Available at most post offices in Canada.

Johnny Chinook
Robert E. Gard
(Edmonton: Hurtig, 1967)
A collection of legends and tall tales from western Canada.

If you would like to read more about the weather, look for these books in the class, school, or local library, or in a bookstore.

Air
David Allen
(Toronto: Annick, 1993)
A look at all aspects of air, including the chinook, cyclones, rainbows, clouds, and the ozone layer. Illustrated by Gordon Bain.

Exploring the Sky by Day
Terence Dickinson
(Camdem East, Ontario: Camden House, 1988)
An illustrated young adult's guide to weather and the atmosphere.

Looking at Weather
David Suzuki and Barbara Henner
(Toronto: Stoddart, 1988)
An illustrated book for young adults by one of Canada's most popular scientists and broadcasters.

Snow
Frank B. Edwards
(Toronto: Firefly, 1992)
A look at all aspects of snow. Illustrated by John Biachi.

The Weather Book
Reuben A. Hornstein
(Toronto: McClelland & Stewart, 1980)
A book on weather folklore and forecasting, written in conjunction with Environment Canada.

Weather Watch
Valerie Wyatt
(Toronto: Greey de Pencier, 1988)
A young adult's book dealing with weather and weather experiments. Illustrated by Pat Cupples.

CHAPTER SIX

How Summer Came to Canada

retold by William Toye

Brian Marion/Gallery Louise Smith

WARM-UP

According to the Micmac people, Glooskap brought summer to Canada. Glooskap is the mythical lord and creator of the Micmac people. Do you know any legends or stories about Glooskap? Share them with the rest of the class.

Skimming

Sometimes we want to have a general idea about a piece of writing before we read it carefully. This activity will show you one way of doing that.

Take one minute (60 seconds) to read the first three paragraphs in the story. This kind of fast reading for the general idea is called skimming. Next, try to answer the following questions. Do not look back at the story to answer them.

1. Who is Glooskap?
2. Where does he live?
3. Who does he meet?
4. Where does Winter live?
5. What happens to the land?
6. What happens to the Indians?
7. How does Glooskap send Winter away?

Remember that, in the legends of First Nations peoples, Winter is not only the coldest season of the year, but also a person who has supernatural powers.

Introduction to the Story

Think about these questions as you read the story: How does Glooskap use his magic powers? Whose magic is stronger: Glooskap's or Winter's? Who helps Glooskap in his struggle against Winter? How does Summer come to Canada? What happens to Winter, Summer, and Glooskap at the end of the story?

How Summer Came to Canada

Long, long ago, when the Indians were first created, the giant° Winter came down from his home in the Far North to live in eastern Canada.

As he breathed on the trees and flowers and passed his icy hand over mountains and fields, all the once-green land became frozen and white.

Nothing grew anywhere and the Indians died from cold and hunger. Glooskap, their lord and creator, decided to use his magic powers to send Winter away.

He went to the beautiful place where Winter lived. The giant's tent glistened° white and cold in the rays of the moon. Above it the sky was filled with flashing, quivering° lights and the stars shone like diamonds.

When Glooskap entered the tent, Winter made him welcome. But before Glooskap could use his magic powers to send Winter away, Winter cast a spell° on him. He proceeded to tell Glooskap tales of ancient times when the whole world was covered with ice and snow. Glooskap forgot the reason for his visit and felt a great longing to stay with Winter. He became drowsy°. He fell into a deep sleep and had a dream.

The giant Winter, looking cold and menacing°, loomed over Glooskap in his dream.

Then suddenly he grew smaller and smaller. The smaller he became the faster the ice and snow melted, until they made raging torrents° of water.

When Winter had all but disappeared and the land turned green again, the dream ended. For six months Glooskap slept like a bear.

When Glooskap woke, his friend Loon° appeared before him. "There is a land far away in the South," he said, "where it is always warm. A Queen reigns° there and her power is greater than the giant Winter's. Go to her and bring her here."

So Glooskap went to the ocean, many miles away, and called for Whale°. He jumped on Whale's back and together they sped through the water for many days, until the ocean became warm and the air sweet with the fragrance of flowers and pines. When Glooskap looked into the clear green depths of the sea and saw white sand beneath him, he slipped off Whale's back and swam ashore.

With great strides° Glooskap walked far inland along a flower-lined road. Tulip trees grew on either side, birds of brilliant plumage° sang in their branches, and wherever flowers or trees did not grow, the ground was covered with velvety grass.

He came to a grove° where he heard voices raised in song. He peered through the trees and saw four maidens° singing and dancing in a Wilderness of Flowers. They held blossoms in their hands and circled around the fairest woman Glooskap had ever seen.

When he recovered from his surprise, Glooskap noticed that a little old woman stood beside him. "Who are these maidens?" he asked her. "The Fairies° of Light and Sunshine and Flowers," the old woman answered. "They dance around their Queen. Her name is Summer."

Glooskap knew that here at last was the Queen who could match old Winter's power. He sang a magic song. When the Queen heard it she willingly left her maidens and went to Glooskap. Unravelling° behind him a slender cord of moosehide°, he raced away with Summer.

After many days Glooskap and Summer reached the Northland°. The people were all asleep; the cold and lonely land was also asleep under Winter's spell.

Winter's tent gleamed in the morning sun. The giant was overjoyed to see Glooskap again. He determined to keep him with him always, and Summer too, by casting his strongest spell.

But the power of Summer was changing the frozen land. Ice and snow were turning to water. New grass and leaves showed that the earth had returned to life.

Even old Winter was melting away. He wept and his tears fell like cold rain on all the land. Summer took pity on him. "I love Glooskap's country and want to stay," she said, "but we cannot live here together. Return to your home in the North for half the year. When you come back, I will never disturb you. But I will rule when you are away."

Winter could do nothing but agree to this. In the Far North he keeps the land in his strong and icy grip° all year round. But he leaves in late autumn and comes back to Glooskap's country where he reigns for half the year.

On his approach, Summer follows Glooskap's moosehide cord to her home in the South and to the Wilderness of Flowers.

But every year her love of Glooskap's country brings her back to awaken the earth from its deep sleep and bestow° life on everything that grows. In this way Winter and Summer divide their rule between them in Glooskap's country.

GLOSSARY

giant (n)	in legends and tales, a very big strong man, often unfriendly and cruel
glistened (v)	shone from (or as if from) a wet surface
quivering (adj)	trembling or shaking a little
cast a spell (exp)	to make something happen or to cause a certain condition to happen by the power of magic
drowsy (adj)	ready to fall asleep
menacing (adj)	threatening
raging torrents (n)	wild and violent rushing streams of water
Loon (n)	a water bird known for its very sad cry; in First Nations legends, the loon is a bird with both natural and supernatural powers
reigns (v)	rules over
Whale (n)	a very large animal that lives in the sea and looks like a fish, but is a mammal; in First Nations legends, the whale is an animal with both natural and supernatural powers

strides (n)	long steps in walking
plumage (n)	a bird's covering of feathers
grove (n)	a small group of trees
maidens (n)	young girls who are not married
Fairies (n)	small imaginary figures with magical powers and shaped like human beings
unravelling (v)	causing something such as thread or cloth to become separated or unwoven
moosehide (n)	the skin of a moose, especially when it has been removed to be used for leather
Northland (n)	in First Nations legends, Northland refers to the cold land in the northern part of North America
grip (n)	a very tight, forceful hold
bestow (v)	to give

There may be other words and expressions in the story that are not familiar to you. Write each one in your journal. Then look it up in a dictionary, ask another student, or ask the teacher for a definition. Write the definition on the line beside the word or expression. Try to use the new word or expression in a sentence.

READING ACTIVITY

Who?

You will probably want to look back and scan the text to decide on the answers to some of these questions. Discuss the answers with the teacher and other students.

1. Who rules over the land in the South?
2. Who slept for six months?
3. Who made the land frozen and white?
4. Who carried Glooskap on his back?
5. Who told Glooskap about the land in the South?
6. Who dances around the Queen?
7. Who lives in a tent?
8. Who does Glooskap love?

LISTENING ACTIVITY

The Micmac

Read the key words and the sentences below. First, listen to the text. Second, listen to the text and, in your journal, fill in the blanks with an appropriate word or expression from the list of key words. You will not use all the words. Third, listen to the text and complete the blanks. Discuss the answers with the teacher and other students.

Key Words
fur
Europe
lakes
Algonquian
farm
rivers
Nova Scotia
fiddler
Micmac
Prince Edward Island
fish
hunt
poet
Newfoundland

1. The language of the Micmac is called _____.
2. Micmac is an Eastern _____ language.
3. Original Micmac settlements were along bays and _____.
4. In the summer, the Micmac would _____.
5. In the winter, the Micmac would _____.
6. The Micmac were among the first aboriginal peoples to meet settlers from _____.
7. The Micmac were once very involved in the _____ trade.
8. Leo Cremo is a fiddler from _____.
9. Rita Joe is a _____ from Prince Edward Island.
10. The Micmac live mainly in the Maritimes, _____, and Quebec.

DISCUSSION AND WRITING ACTIVITIES

Retell the Legend

Imagine that you are Winter or Summer. From that point of view, retell the legend of *How Summer Came to Canada* either orally or in writing.

First Nations Legends

Have you ever heard or read about an aboriginal legend? Talk or write about it with the teacher and other students. Then decide who has heard or read the most compelling legend.

Create a Legend

Create and develop your own legend. It could be about one of these topics:

- how day and night came about
- why the monkey has a long tail
- where the moon and the stars came from

Share your legend with the teacher and other students. Then decide who has told or written the most interesting one.

First Nations Hunters of Eastern Canada

Choose one of these First Nations groups of Eastern Woodlands Hunters: (1) Abenaki, (2) Algonquian, (3) Maliseet, (4) Micmac, (5) Nipissing, (6) Ojibwa, or (7) Ottawa.

Find out some information about the group, such as its history, territory, language, food, shelter, clothing, transportation, social and political organization, religion, art and leisure, or contemporary life.

Talk or write about the First Nations people that you have researched. In your opinion, what is the most interesting aspect of their culture?

LIBRARY BOOKS

If you would like to read other stories by William Toye, look for the following books in the class, school, or local library, or in a bookstore.

How Summer Came to Canada
(Toronto: Oxford, 1969)
This edition is illustrated by Elizabeth Cleaver.

The Loon's Necklace
(Toronto: Oxford, 1977)
A Tsimshian legend retold by William Toye. This edition is illustrated by Elizabeth Cleaver.

Cartier Discovers the St. Lawrence
(Toronto: Oxford, 1970)
A book for young adults about the early French explorer Jacques Cartier. Illustrated by Laszlo Gal.

If you would like to read other stories about Glooskap, look for the following books in the class, school, or local library, or in a bookstore.

Canadian Wonder Tales
Cyrus Macmillan
(Toronto: Bodley Head, 1974)
A collection of 58 folktales and folk songs of Canada.

Glooskap and His Magic
Kay Hill
(Toronto: McClelland & Stewart, 1963)
A collection of 19 stories about Glooskap.

How Glooskap Outwits the Ice Giants
Howard Norman
(Boston: Little, Brown, 1989)
A collection of six stories about Glooskap.

More Glooskap Stories
Kay Hill
(Toronto: McClelland & Stewart, 1970)
A collection of 18 stories about Glooskap.

If you would like to read more about the Micmac people, look for the following books in the class, school, or local library, or in a bookstore.

The Micmac
Ruth Holmes Whitehead and Harold McGee
(Halifax: Nimbus, 1983)
A look at the life of the Micmac 500 years ago, before the arrival of European settlers.

Micmac by Choice
Mary Olga McKenna
(Toronto: Lorimer, 1990)
A biography of Elsie Sark, a Micmac woman from Prince Edward Island.

Micmac Legends of Prince Edward Island
J. J. Sark
(Charlottetown: Ragweed, 1988)
A collection of legends with illustrations by Michael Francis and George Paul.

The Micmacs
Robert Leavitt
(Toronto: Fitzhenry & Whiteside, 1985)
An illustrated history of the Micmacs.

Winter of the Black Weasel
Tom Dawe
(St. John's: Breakwater, 1988)
An illustrated book for young adults based on a Newfoundland Micmac legend.

CHAPTER SEVEN

Raven and the Whale

retold by Ronald Melzack

Brian Marion/Gallery Louise Smith

WARM-UP

Look at the picture carefully. This is Raven, a magical being who can transform himself into other animals. He is a creature who likes playing tricks on people and animals. Raven legends come from the many First Nations groups on the west coast of British Columbia.

Scanning Two Different Sources of Information

For this activity, you will scan the texts in Chapter Six and Chapter Seven.

After you read each question below, quickly scan the two legends. Find the answers to the questions. You do not need to find any other information as you read. Try to do this activity in less than three minutes.

1. Who is Raven?
2. How is Raven like Glooskap?
3. Where do Glooskap and Raven live?
4. Who are the beautiful women that Glooskap and Raven meet?
5. Where do these beautiful women live?

Think about these questions as you read the story: How does Raven feel about the woman he meets? What does he want to do? How does the woman respond to Raven? Why? What does Raven do? What happens to the woman? Why?

*R*aven and the Whale

One evening, while the sun was setting, Raven flew along the seashore to watch the ever-changing° colors of the waves. As he scanned the horizon, he caught sight of fountains of water rising up from the distant sea. The water shot up high, foamed and bubbled, and fell back on the sea. Raven was curious and flew toward the sparkling, foaming fountains. Soon he was close enough to see a school° of whales, each whale spouting° a stream of bubbly water.

Raven soared above the whales and, to his surprise, saw a faint glow of light coming from one of the whales each time it opened its mouth. He flew closer to the whale to see where the light came from. Each time the whale's mouth opened, Raven flew a little closer — the light was mysterious, yet it looked warm and inviting. Just as Raven was inspecting the light, the whale lurched° forward and swallowed him.

Raven looked around. The whale's spine° above him resembled a strong and beautiful roof, and the delicate ribs° formed graceful arches, like the walls of a great house. He listened, and heard the rhythmic beat of the whale's heart. Raven lifted his beak° and walked swiftly toward the light, his wing-cape° swirling behind him. Then he stopped suddenly in astonishment°. In the center of the whale was a softly glowing lamp, and beside the lamp stood the most beautiful girl he had ever seen. The dancing flame-light° made her face glow, and Raven was enchanted°.

The girl looked at Raven and smiled shyly. Raven moved closer. The lamp flame fluttered ceaselessly° — it rose and fell, rose and fell. Its dancing light radiated warmth and beauty, and the girl's white teeth dazzled Raven's eyes as he watched her. When he approached a little, Raven saw that the girl was dancing on her toes. Her legs barely moved, while her body and arms swayed slowly in rhythm to the loud beats of the whale's heart. Raven watched her supple°, graceful movements, and noticed that the tips of her toes flowed from a delicate thread that was attached to the whale's beating heart.

Raven was overwhelmed with love for the girl as he watched her dance.

Finally, Raven asked, "Who are you?"

"I am the whale's spirit," said the girl.

"I love you," said Raven. "Come with me and be my wife."

The girl laughed sweetly, and her laughter echoed through the whale.

"I cannot leave," she said, dancing while she talked. "The whale and I are one, and I must look after the lamp. It warms us and keeps us alive in the freezing water."

"But you are too beautiful to spend your life inside a whale, dancing every moment, yet never moving anywhere."

"I am the whale's spirit," said the girl, "and I cannot leave. Besides, I love this lamp, and it makes me happy."

"Then take the lamp with you," said Raven.

"No," said the girl. "The lamp must stay where it is, and you must never touch it." She smiled at Raven and continued. "I am pleased to have a friend, and you may stay as long as you wish. But you must never, never touch my lamp."

Raven watched the girl, and a deep sadness overcame him. "How beautiful she is," he thought to himself. "How graceful and delicate and sweet. How happy I would be if she became my wife!"

As Raven looked around, he saw an opening above him. It was the whale's spout, and Raven could see the stars when he looked straight through it. Slowly, a plan formed in his mind.

When the whale began to sleep in the still blackness of the night, the girl's dance became slower and sleepier. Her eyelids shut from time to time°, and she seemed to sleep even while she danced. Raven waited, watching — then, the moment her eyes closed, he snatched up° the lamp of life, swept the girl into his arms, and snapped her free from the delicate thread. He dashed° toward the spout.

But too late!

The whale suddenly lurched up and thrashed° around. Raven and the girl fell backwards. The lamp flickered°, grew fainter, and died out. Raven held the girl tightly in his arms, but she became smaller and lost her shape. She no longer moved and became tinier° and tinier.

"Come back to me!" he called. "I will make you my wife and look after you as long as you live."

But Raven heard only the sea waves swirling around him as the girl vanished into nothingness.

The whale suddenly stopped moving. Raven looked up and saw the sky through the whale's spout. He lowered his beak and flew up, and in a moment he was high above the whale. It was dead, and had washed up on shore. Raven flew down to the shore, sat on a rock, and looked at the whale.

"How beautiful is the spirit of a whale," he whispered to himself.

White-capped° waves rushed up on shore. The salty mist made Raven's eyes smart°, and tears rolled down his face as he stared at the whale. He watched it for many hours as it rocked gently back and forth with the inrushing and outgoing tide.

GLOSSARY

ever-changing (adj)	always different
a **school** (of whales) (n)	a large group of one kind of fish or certain sea animals swimming together
spouting (adj)	throwing liquid or liquid coming out in a forceful stream from a **spout** or opening
lurched (v)	moved in an irregular and sudden way
spine (n)	the row of bones down the centre of the back of humans and some animals
ribs (n)	the 12 pairs of bones running around the chest of humans or animals, from the spine to where they join at the front
beak (n)	the hard, horny mouth of a bird
wing-cape (n)	Raven's wings or the limbs by which a bird flies; the wings look like a cape, a loose outer garment without sleeves that is fastened at the neck and hangs from the shoulder
astonishment (n)	great surprise or wonder
flame-light (n)	a bright, strong, burning light from a candle
enchanted (adj)	filled with delight

ceaselessly (adv)	unending; continuously; without stopping
supple (adj)	bending or moving easily, especially in the joints of the body
from time to time (exp)	occasionally; now and again
snatched up (v)	got hold of hastily and forcefully
dashed (v)	ran quickly and suddenly
thrashed (v)	moved wildly about
flickered (v)	burned or moved unsteadily
tinier (adj)	much smaller
white-capped (adj)	a whitish mass of bubbles or foam on the surface or the top of ocean waves
smart (adj)	to cause or feel a painful stinging sensation, usually not lasting long

There may be other words and expressions in the story that are not familiar to you. Write each one in your journal. Then look it up in a dictionary, ask another student, or ask the teacher for a definition. Write the definition on the line beside the word or expression. Try to use the new word or expression in a sentence.

READING ACTIVITY

Guess the Meaning of Words from Context

Following is a list of words from the text. Choose an appropriate word or expression for each blank in the sentences below. You will not use all the words. Discuss the answers with the teacher and other students.

a) fountains

b) lamp

c) ribs

d) a school

e) the sea

f) spine

g) spirit

h) spout

i) the stars

j) thread

k) toes

l) wife

1. The whale's _____ were like the walls of a house.
2. One day while flying, Raven saw _____ of water.
3. A _____ was attached to the whale's heart.
4. The light in the whale came from a _____.
5. The girl was the whale's _____.
6. Raven could see _____ through the whale's spout.
7. The girl would dance on her _____.
8. The Raven wanted the girl to be his _____.

LISTENING ACTIVITY

Raven Legends

First, listen to the text. Second, listen and write **T** in your journal if the sentence is true according to the text, **F** if the sentence is false according to the text, and **DS** if the text doesn't say. Third, listen to the text and complete the activity. Discuss the answers with the teacher and other students.

1. Raven legends come from British Columbia.
2. Canoes were used for exploring.
3. Canoes are painted by women.
4. The totem pole was never placed near water.
5. Families made their own totem poles
6. The First Nations population of British Columbia is 70 000.

DISCUSSION AND WRITING ACTIVITIES

Create a Legend

Imagine that the sentences below are the beginning of your own legend. Create and develop the middle and the end of it. Share your legend with the teacher and other students.

One evening, while the sun was setting, I walked along the seashore to watch the ever-changing colours of the waves. As I scanned the sand, the rocks, and the sea, I caught sight of X. I was curious and walked toward it. Soon I was close enough to see…

Fish Stories

A "fish story" is like a tall tale or a wildly exaggerated story. In your own words, talk or write about one of the following "fish stories":

- a whale that swallowed a person whole, such as Jonah or Pinocchio
- a fish that swallowed a treasure, such as a ring or money
- a person who struggled to catch a big fish and finally caught it
- a person who tried to catch a fish but didn't succeed

Whale Watching

Some companies organize trips for people to go "whale watching," so that they can see a school of whales in its natural habitat. Inquire at a travel agency, a tourist information centre, or a marine biology institution to discover if there are whale watches in your area. If so, find out as much information about them as possible.

Beached Whales

From time to time, whales swim out of the water, land on a beach, and die. People often try to get them back in the water, but they do not always succeed. Investigate this phenomenon and try to find out as much information as possible about why whales do this, and how people can help to save beached whales.

Information About Whales

Write a letter to one of these organizations: World Wildlife Fund Canada, Environment Canada, or the National Geographic Society. Your teacher will provide you with the addresses and postal codes.

Ask the organization for information about whales in Canada and North America. When you receive the information, read it carefully. Did you learn any other facts about whales? What are they?

Northwest Coast First Nations

The Northwest Coast peoples lived diverse lives, based on the resources of the sea. Their culture presents many powerful images: tall totem poles, great war canoes, and great feasts called potlatches. Yet these images can only begin to describe the rich variety of their cultures.

Choose one of these groups of Northwest Coast First Nations: (1) Bella Coola,

(2) Coast Salish, (3) Haida, (4) Haisla, (5) Kwakiutl, (6) Nootka, (7) Tlingit, or (8) Tsimshian.

Find out some information about the group, such as its history, territory, language, food, shelter, clothing, transportation, social and political organization, religion, art and leisure, or contemporary life.

Talk or write about the First Nations people that you have researched. In your opinion, what is the most interesting aspect of their culture?

LIBRARY BOOKS

If you would like to read other works by Ronald Melzack, look for the following books in the class, school, or local library, or in a bookstore.

Raven, Creator of the World
Ronald Melzack
(Toronto: McClelland & Stewart, 1970)
A collection of Raven stories, including "Raven and the Whale." Written for young adults with illustrations by Laszlo Gal.

The Day Tuk Became a Hunter and Other Eskimo Stories
Ronald Melzack
(Toronto: McClelland & Stewart, 1967)
A collection of legends written for young adults. Illustrated by Carol Jones.

Why the Man in the Moon Is Happy and Other Eskimo Creation Stories
Ronald Melzack
(Toronto: McClelland & Stewart, 1977)
A collection of legends written for young adults. Illustrated by Laszlo Gal.

If you would like to read more legends about Raven, look for the following books in the class, school, or local library, or in a bookstore.

How Raven Freed the Moon
Anne Cameron
(Maderia Park, British Columbia: Harbour, 1985)
A First Nations legend retold for young adults, with illustrations by Tara Miller.

Raven Steals the Light
Robert Bringhurst and Bill Reid
(Vancouver: Douglas & McIntyre, 1988)
Haida Raven legends written for adults. Illustrated by Bill Reid.

Sketko the Raven
Robert Ayre
(Toronto: Macmillan, 1961)
A collection of Raven legends. Illustrated by Philip Surrey.

If you would like to read works of related interest, look for the following books in the class, school, or local library, or in a bookstore.

Birds of Canada
W. Earl Godfrey
(Ottawa: National Museum of Canada, 1986)
A very large and detailed guide to birds that are native to Canada. Illustrated by John A. Crosby and S. D. MacDonald.

Houses of Wood
Bonnie Shemie
(Montreal: Tundra, 1992)
An illustrated look at the traditional First Nations dwellings of the Northwest Coast.

CHAPTER EIGHT

The Magnificent Voyage of Emily Carr

JOVETTE MARCHESSAULT
translated by Linda Gaboriau

Metro Toronto Reference Library (T31407).

WARM-UP

Look at the picture carefully. This is Emily Carr. She is a famous Canadian. Do you know why she is famous? Have you ever seen any of her work? Tell the class about it.

Scanning for Specific Information

Sometimes we scan a piece of writing to find a few facts. We don't read everything. We don't even need to get a general idea about the piece of writing. We need only the specific pieces of information. We do this by reading very quickly.

In this activity, you will try to answer the questions below by scanning the brief biography of Emily Carr. Try to answer each question in ten seconds or less.

1. Where and when was Emily Carr born?
2. In which countries did she study art?
3. Which objects did she begin to paint in her 30s?
4. Where did she go in 1927?
5. Who did she meet?
6. Which painter encouraged her?
7. What was the name of her first book?

Biography

Emily Carr was born in Victoria, British Columbia, in 1871. She studied art in the United States and England. In her 30s, she began painting the villages and totem poles of Northwest Coast First Nations. Although these paintings are recognized as some of the finest examples of Canadian art, they were largely ignored at the time. In 1913, she was forced to open up a boarding house in order to support herself.

Serious recognition of Carr's work did not take place until 1927, when some of her paintings were exhibited at a national show in Ottawa. It was at this point in her life that she first met Lawren Harris and other members of the Group of Seven. Their encouragement and support helped bring her talent into the public eye.

In 1937, Carr suffered a severe heart attack. Her health continued to decline in the years that followed, and the artist turned increasingly to writing as a means of artistic expression. Her first book, *Klee Wyck*, dealt with her experiences visiting First Nations villages. Published in 1941, the work received a Governor General's Award for non-fiction. Other books followed, including *Growing Pains*, published in 1946, a year after her death.

Introduction to the Play

Here are two scenes from a play about the life of Emily Carr. In the first scene, Emily Carr is still a young but talented painter. She "talks" to a painting by A. Y. Jackson, a famous member of the Group of Seven. In the second scene, she talks to Lawren Harris, another member of the Group of Seven, who recognizes her talent and encourages her.

It is important to remember that two of the three characters in the play are artists. They are talking about works of art, and the language they use is "artistic."

Think about these questions as you read the scenes from the play: What are Emily Carr's feelings in the first scene? What are her feelings at the end of the second scene?

$\mathcal{T}$he Magnificent Voyage of Emily Carr

(Scene 1)

The Group of Seven studio in Toronto. A place where the artists meet, work and exhibit. There are several canvases hanging on the wall; they are relatively small and signed Jackson. EMILY goes over to the paintings and studies them attentively, with true enjoyment.

EMILY	(*speaking to the paintings*) I'm particularly fond of your snow scenes of Quebec, Mr. Jackson.
JACKSON PAINTING	That's very kind of you. Are you a connoisseur°, Mrs. ...?
EMILY	Carr, Emily Carr.
JACKSON PAINTING	Oh, yes! Emile Carr, the West Coast painter. Your husband is quite talented, Mrs. Carr.
EMILY	I am the painter! And I'm nobody's wife.
JACKSON PAINTING	(*astonished*) A woman painter?
EMILY	A man painter and a woman painter — that makes a pair!
JACKSON PAINTING	You never know what to expect with women. And when you do, it's even worse! (*He laughs, EMILY is furious.*)

(Scene 2)

EMILY CARR takes a sketch pad°, a piece of charcoal and prepares to do a drawing, a sketch of the totem poles....LAWREN HARRIS enters with a painting under his arm. His face lights up when he sees Emily.

HARRIS	Emily Carr! I am Lawren Harris, from the Group of Seven. I like your work — I am struck° by its power and inspiration°. Every

time I look at your paintings, they cleanse my eyes and my heart, they make me want to paint, they make me want to outdo myself! (*solemn, with emotion*) Emily Carr, you are one of us.

EMILY   (*visibly moved*) I'll never forget what you just said.

HARRIS   What do you think of Jackson's paintings?

EMILY   Whenever I look at Mr. Jackson's paintings, the same thought springs to mind°: this painter does not come from the West Coast.

HARRIS   The vast° spaces of your land do not inhabit his paintings.

EMILY   He doesn't paint the giant trees that reveal all the forces of the Earth, nor does he paint the rolling clouds, or our rivers that swell with the rains and hurl° salmon into the azure° skies!

HARRIS   Your mountains that tower over everything, with their slopes° glazed like Chinese pottery°!

EMILY   Everything Mr. Jackson paints is very small. But his paintings are better than mine. He takes liberties I would never dream of.

HARRIS   But when I compare your paintings with his, to me it is obvious that yours have something his are lacking°.

EMILY   Love for the people and for this country.

HARRIS   That's exactly what it is — your paintings are full of love, and beauty!

EMILY   If I put love and beauty into my work, it's probably because I feel pity for this beauty which must die.

HARRIS   Does beauty die because that is the law of all matter, or because of the way we paint it? (*beat*) Love plus beauty, plus pity — that's the closest we can come to a definition of art.

EMILY   Art should not be defined. It is made of vitality and youth and it can only die by accident. There is no law of death or decrepitude° for Art!

HARRIS   I want to show you my most recent painting. I need to know your opinion of it.

EMILY   (*touched and a bit amazed to be asked for her opinion*) My opinion? (*She looks at the painting.*) It is incredibly powerful! Does it have a title?

HARRIS   (*very moved by EMILY's admiration*) "Above Lake Superior."

EMILY   My eyes have always longed to gaze° upon a painting like that.

HARRIS	What do you think of it?
EMILY	I think this painting is the accomplished fruit of an inner effort.
HARRIS	Emily, the first time I laid eyes on your work, I thought it was beyond anything I had ever seen before. Your paintings are permeated° with life. You paint images! Bursts of light! It feels as if you submit your entire being to the power of colour. The way you paint the Amerindian totem poles — you place them on a pedestal of phosphorescence°, between two wings of light. Even if they come from the ancient soul of humanity, your paintings have such incredible youth!
EMILY	(*She looks for somewhere to sit because she feels dizzy.*) Help me.
HARRIS	(*worried, he takes her in his arms*) Do you feel ill?
EMILY	(*she bursts out laughing*) I've never felt better in my life! In the last few minutes, I've heard more stimulating things than I've heard in over fifty years in Victoria. (*She steps back.*)
HARRIS	(*he raises his arms, his hands outstretched*) Let's salute the energy of true encounters°!
EMILY	Let's salute the Group of Seven! The revolution! The public's incomprehension and the conservative critics' insults will be our crowning glory°.
HARRIS	The materialistic 20th Century follows the straight and narrow°. Fortunately the winding, sometimes tortuous° routes are those of the artists.

GLOSSARY

connoisseur (n)	a person with a good understanding of a subject, especially art or a matter of taste
sketch pad (n)	a number of sheets of paper fastened together, used for drawing rough pictures or sketches
struck (v)	impressed by
inspiration (n)	(something which causes) an urge to produce good and beautiful things, especially works of art
springs to mind (exp)	occurs quickly and suddenly in one's thoughts
vast (adj)	very large and wide; great in size and amount

hurl (v)	throw with force
azure (adj)	bright blue, as of the sky
slopes (n)	surfaces that lie at angles or in a sloping direction
pottery (n)	(objects made out of) baked clay
lacking (adj)	not present; missing
decrepitude (n)	weakness or bad condition due to old age
gaze (v)	look steadily for a long or short period of time
permeated (v)	passed through or into every part of (something)
phosphorescence (n)	the giving out of light with little or no heat
encounters (n)	meetings, especially those that are unexpected or dangerous
crowning glory (exp)	great fame or success; praise or honour
straight and narrow (exp)	a conservative way of thinking and acting according to the conventions of proper and respectable society
tortuous (adj)	twisted; unconventional

READING ACTIVITY

Inference Questions

Sometimes you can find information in a story that is not stated clearly in the words. You infer the information — that is, you make a logical guess — from either what is in the text, or your knowledge of the world, or both.

Try to infer the probable answers to the questions below by looking at the story. Be ready to give your reasons.

1. Why does the Jackson painting think that Emily Carr is the wife of a painter?
2. Why does Lawren Harris like Emily Carr's paintings?
3. How does Emily Carr know that Jackson is not a West Coast painter?
4. How does Emily Carr compare herself to Jackson?
5. Why does Lawren Harris want Emily Carr's opinion of his most recent painting?
6. How does Emily Carr feel about her conversation with Lawren Harris?
7. How do Harris and Carr feel about the life of the public and the life of an artist?

LISTENING ACTIVITY

Interactive Dictation

An interactive dictation is similar to a dictation, but the texts are dictated by students to students.

An interactive dictation is done in pairs. One member of the pair is Student A and the other member is Student B. Student A is the only one who looks at the text marked Student A, and Student B is the only one who looks at the text marked Student B.

Student A takes the first turn. Student A dictates a text on the Group of Seven to Student B. That is, Student A will read the text first, read the text with pauses a second time, and then read the text a third time.

Student B takes the second turn. Student B dictates a text on the life of Tom Thomson to Student A. That is, Student B will read the text three times, following the procedure described for Student A.

In order to correct the interactive dictation, Student A looks at Student B's journal and Student B looks at Student A's journal. Discuss the corrections with the teacher and other students.

STUDENT A

Read to Student B

The Group of Seven was a group of artists who focused mainly on painting landscapes. The original members were Lawren Harris, A. Y. Jackson, Franklin Carmichael, Franz Johnston, Arthur Lismer, J. E. H. MacDonald, and F. H. Varley.

All were friends, most having met each other through their work as commercial artists. A strong influence on the group was the work of Tom Thomson, another commercial artist and friend. A lover of the outdoors, he had encouraged the members of the group to explore the possibilities of painting the Canadian landscape. Thomson was never a member of the group, having died three years before its foundation in 1920.

The goal of the Group of Seven was to capture the spirit of Canada in their art. In order to do this, they organized many trips into the Canadian wilderness, sketching and painting nature in its different seasons. Many sketches were either finished or redone in the artists' studios.

Throughout the group's existence, changes in membership took place. In 1926, Franz Johnston resigned and was replaced by A. J. Casson. In the early 1930s, Edward Holgate and L. L. Fitzgerald were also admitted.

Although it disbanded in 1933, just 13 years after its formation, the Group of Seven remains the most famous group of Canadian painters.

STUDENT A

Write in Your Journal

Tom Thomson

Tom Thomson was born in 1887 in rural Ontario. He grew up on a farm with his parents and _____ brothers and sisters. He took his first art lesson in _____ , and got a job as a commercial artist the following _____ with Grip Limited in Toronto. It was at this company _____ he met and became friends with other artists who would _____ day form the Group of Seven.

In 1912, Thomson's career _____ a dramatic change. He travelled to Algonquin Park, sketching and _____ its landscape for the very first time. After returning, he _____ his work to create one of his most famous paintings, "_____ Lake." The painting was bought the following year by the _____ of Ontario. The sale brought Thomson $250 at a _____ when he was earning just 75 cents an hour.

In _____ fall of 1913, Thomson met James MacCallum, a medical doctor _____ a great love of art. MacCallum offered to pay Thomson's _____ for one year so that he could concentrate on his _____. Thomson accepted and left his job as a commercial artist. _____ the few remaining years of his life, Thomson spent three _____ a year travelling about Algonquin Park. In the winters, he _____ return to Toronto, where he reworked many of his sketches _____ finished paintings.

In 1917, Thomson disappeared while on a canoe _____ . His body was found eight days later.

Read to Student A

Tom Thomson was born in 1887 in rural Ontario. He grew up on a farm with his parents and eight brothers and sisters. He took his first art lesson in 1906, and got a job as a commercial artist the following year with Grip Limited in Toronto. It was at this company that he met and became friends with other artists who would one day form the Group of Seven.

In 1912, Thomson's career began a dramatic change. He travelled to Algonquin Park, sketching and painting its landscape for the very first time. After returning, he used his work to create one of his most famous paintings, "Northern Lake." The painting was bought the following year by the government of Ontario. The sale brought Thomson $250 at a time when he was earning just 75 cents an hour.

In the fall of 1913, Thomson met James MacCallum, a medical doctor with a great love of art. MacCallum offered to pay Thomson's expenses for one year so that he could concentrate on his art. Thomson accepted and left his job as a commercial artist. During the few remaining years of his life, Thomson spent three seasons a year travelling about Algonquin Park. In the winters, he would return to Toronto, where he reworked many of his sketches into finished paintings.

In 1917, Thomson disappeared while on a canoe trip. His body was found eight days later.

STUDENT B

Write in Your Journal

The Group of Seven

The Group of Seven was a group of artists who focused mainly on painting landscapes. The original members were Lawren Harris, A. Y. _____ , Franklin Carmichael, Franz Johnston, Arthur Lismer, J. E. H. _____ , and F. H. Varley.

All were friends, _____ having met each other through their work as _____ artists. A strong influence on the group was the _____ of Tom Thomson, another commercial artist and _____ . A lover of the outdoors, he had _____ the members of the group to explore the possibilities _____ painting the Canadian landscape. Thomson was never a _____ of the group, having died three years before _____ foundation in 1920.

The goal of the Group of _____ was to capture the spirit of Canada _____ their art. In order to do this, they _____ many trips into the Canadian wilderness, sketching and _____ nature in its different seasons. Many sketches were _____ finished or redone in the artists' studios.

Throughout the group's _____ , changes in membership took place. In 1926, Franz Johnston resigned and was replaced _____ A. J. Casson. In the early 1930s, Edward _____ and L. L. Fitzgerald were also admitted.

Although _____ disbanded in 1933, just 13 years after its formation, the Group of Seven remains the most famous group of Canadian painters.

DISCUSSION AND WRITING ACTIVITIES

East Coast, West Coast

Find out some information about the people, places, things, animals, and events on the East Coast and the West Coast of Canada. In your opinion, are there more differences or more similarities?

A Definition of Art

In the play, Lawren Harris says that, "Love plus beauty, plus pity — that's the closest we can come to a definition of art." Emily Carr says, "Art should not be defined." Do you agree with both artists or with neither artist? What is your definition of art?

Your Favourite Canadian Artist

Choose your favourite Canadian artist. Do some research and find out some information about his or her life or work. Then talk or write about your favourite artist with the teacher and other students in the class. You can choose an artist from the list below, or any other Canadian artist whose work you admire.

Maurice Cullen

Thomas Davies

Marc-Aurèle de Foy Suzor-Coté

Lionel LeMoine FitzGerald

John Fraser

Prudence Heward

Edwin Holgate

Paul Kane

Cornelius Krieghoff

William Kurelek

Ozias Leduc

Pegi Nicol MacLeod

David Milne

J.W. Morrice

Jessie Oonark

Paul Peel

Antoine Plamondon

Goodridge Roberts

Carl Schaefer

Homer Watson

Modern Art

The National Gallery in Ottawa is an art museum for all Canadians and visitors to Canada. It is paid for by the federal government of Canada. In other words, money for the National Gallery comes from the taxes that Canadians pay.

Imagine that the National Gallery has a certain sum of money to spend on a work or works for the modern and contemporary art sections of the museum. The director of the museum is sensitive about public opinion, so she has asked people to express their likes and dislikes and preferences for the work or works that the museum will buy.

Choose one of the modern or contemporary artists below. Do some research and find out some information about the life of the artist and his or her work. Then talk or write about your choice with the teacher and other students in the class. Write a letter to the director of the National Gallery expressing your likes, dislikes, and preferences.

Paul-Émile Borduas
Bertram Brooker
Alex Colville
Joseph Drapell
Cathie Falk
Betty Goodwin
Kenojuak Ashevak
Dorothy Knowles
John Lyman
Guido Molinari
Alfred Pellan
Christopher Pratt
Mary Pratt
Jean-Paul Riopelle
Jack Shadbolt
Michael Snow
Joyce Wieland

LIBRARY BOOKS

If you would like to read other works by Jovette Marchessault, look for the following books in the class, school, or local library, or in a bookstore.

The Magnificent Voyage of Emily Carr
(Vancouver: Talonbooks, 1992)
The play from which this excerpt was taken. Originally published as *Le voyage magnifique d'Emily Carr*, this translation is by Linda Gaboriau.

Saga of the Wet Hens
(Vancouver: Talonbooks, 1983)
A feminist play for four women. Originally performed in French as *La saga des poules mouillées*, this translation is by Linda Gaboriau.

Like a Child of the Earth
(Vancouver: Talonbooks, 1988)
Originally published in French as *Comme une enfant de la terre*, this novel was the winner of the 1976 Prix France-Québec. Translated by Yvonne M. Klein, it is the first volume in Marchessault's autobiographical trilogy, *Le crachat solaire*.

Mother of the Grass
(Vancouver: Talonbooks, 1989)
The second volume in the author's *Le crachat solaire* trilogy. Originally published in French as *La mère des herbes*, this translation is by Yvonne M. Klein.

White Pebbles in the Dark Forests
(Vancouver: Talonbooks, 1990)
The final volume in the author's *Le crachat solaire* trilogy. Originally published in French as *Des cailloux blancs pour les forêts obscures*, this translation is by Yvonne M. Klein.

If you would like to read more about Emily Carr, the Group of Seven, and Tom Thomson, look for the following books in the class, school, or local library, or in a bookstore.

The Art of Emily Carr
Doris Shadbolt
(Vancouver: Douglas & McIntyre, 1979)
A collection of Carr's work spanning her entire career.

The Best of the Group of Seven
Joan Murray
(Edmonton: Hurtig, 1984)
A brief collection of some of the artists' best-known works.

The Best of Tom Thomson
Joan Murray
(Edmonton: Hurtig, 1986)
A brief collection of some of the artist's best-known works.

Emily Carr Omnibus
Emily Carr
(Vancouver: Douglas & McIntyre, 1993)
The complete collection of Emily Carr's writings, with an introduction by Doris Shadbolt.

Painters
Kate Taylor
(Toronto: Fitzhenry & Whiteside, 1989)
An illustrated book written for young adults concerning the lives and works of Emily Carr, Tom Thomson, William Kurelek, and Norval Morrisseau.

CHAPTER NINE

The Fire Stealer

retold by William Toye

Brian Marion/Gallery Louise Smith

WARM-UP

Look at the picture carefully. This boy has magic powers. He can change himself into a rabbit. He can also do other magic tricks. He can change leaves from green to red, yellow, and orange. This legend is a very old way of explaining how autumn began in Canada.

Skimming

Look over the following questions. Then skim the story. Read only the first sentence of each paragraph. Next, return to the questions below and write answers to them in no more than five minutes. Do not reread. Write only from memory. Compare your answers with those of another student.

1. Who is Nokomis?
2. Who is Nanabozho?
3. What did people need for heat and cooking?
4. Who brought fire to the world?
5. At what time of the year was Nokomis cold?
6. Where did Nanabozho go?
7. Who was the rabbit?
8. What did Nanabozho take?
9. Who did Nanabozho give it to?
10. How was Nanabozho remembered?

Introduction to the Story

Think about these questions as you read the story: How did Nanabozho change himself into plants and animals? Why were people frightened of fire? How did Nanabozho bring fire to his people? How did they learn to use fire properly?

The Fire Stealer

Long ago an Indian boy lived with his grandmother Nokomis. He was the son of the West Wind° and could do many wonderful things. As a hungry baby he once turned himself into a rabbit so that he could eat grass. Nokomis cradled° him in her arms and named him Nanabozho, her little rabbit.

When Nanabozho grew older, he often changed himself into other things. Once, to trick a friend who was looking for him, he raised his arms, closed his eyes, and thought hard about becoming a tree. Soon roots grew out of his feet and burrowed° into the ground.

Then leaves sprang out of his hands. His body turned into white bark, his arms into branches that sprouted more leaves. Nanabozho had turned into a slender birch°.

In those early days the people had no fire to warm them or to cook their food. They were afraid of fire because they had seen lightning strike a tree and send it up in flames.

The flames spread quickly, and the forest would have burned to the ground if rain had not put out the blaze.

Once a magician went to the underworld° and brought back a fiery torch°. It frightened the people and they would not keep it even for a day. They ordered a young brave° to take it to an old warrior° who lived far away and would watch over it. Every so often the brave returned to the warrior's wigwam° to steal the torch for himself. But it was always well guarded by the old man and his daughter.

One chilly day in autumn Nanabozho found Nokomis huddled° in her blanket, looking miserable. "I've brought you some deer meat," he said, hoping to cheer her up°. But the raw meat was tough, and Nokomis could eat only a little of it with the few teeth she had left. As Nanabozho watched her, his heart filled with pity. He decided that she needed fire to warm her and to cook her food. He would steal it from the warrior, the guardian of the torch.

Nanabozho set out in his canoe° for the place where the warrior lived. He had to paddle for many days before he caught sight of the warrior's wigwam.

After hiding his canoe in the rushes°, he wondered how he could enter the wigwam and steal the torch. An idea occurred to him. "If I change myself into a rabbit," he thought, "the old man's daughter will find me and take me in."

Nanabozho crept towards the wigwam. When he reached the edge of the clearing, he turned himself into a rabbit and hopped closer.

Before long a girl stepped out. She saw the small trembling° animal and picked it up. Crooning° to it and rubbing behind its ears, she carried it inside the lodge°.

The girl's father, who had been sleeping, woke up as she entered. "Where did that rabbit come from?" he growled. "I found him outside," the girl answered. "Good. We'll have rabbit for supper. It will make a tasty meal." He yawned and went back to sleep.

The girl wanted to keep the rabbit as a pet, but she knew better than to disobey her father. With a heavy heart she put the animal near the fire and went to find a knife. Suddenly the rabbit vanished° and an Indian brave stood in its place. The girl was so surprised that she could do nothing but watch as he seized° the torch and dashed from the lodge.

The girl rushed after him. "Come back, you thief!" she cried. "Give us back our fire!"

"Here it is!" yelled Nanabozho and plunged the burning torch into the dry grass. It caught fire and the wind carried the flames and smoke back towards the girl.

The flames rose higher and higher as they spread from one tree to the next. The heat became unbearable° and the girl had to give up the chase.

Nanabozho fastened the torch to the front of his canoe and departed. As he paddled swiftly away, a wonderful sight met his eyes.

He saw that the fire was casting its light over all the maples and birch trees he passed. They glowed with beautiful fiery colors.

When Nanabozho reached home, Nokomis received the gift of fire joyfully. She basked° in the heat it gave and ate her meat with ease, now that it could be cooked.

The people found that fire warmed them when they were cold and made their food more delicious to eat. They soon lost their fear of it when they learned that if they always watched over fire, and did not touch it, it would do them no harm.

Nanabozho was proud of himself for bringing fire to the Indians and wanted to be remembered for what he had done. When autumn came the next year, he made the woods blaze with flaming colors. "Remember me, Nanabozho!" he shouted as he worked his magic on the trees. "Remember how I brought fire to my people!" His people did remember Nanabozho and his gift. Even today he is not forgotten because every year the frosts of autumn turn green leaves red and gold and bronze and yellow — the colors of fire.

GLOSSARY

West Wind (n) soft and gentle moving air from the direction of the west; in aboriginal legends, the West Wind is a character with supernatural powers

cradled (v) held gently as if in a cradle or small bed for a baby

burrowed (v) dug a hole

birch (n) a tree with smooth wood and thin branches

underworld (n) in ancient legends, the place where the spirits of the dead live

torch (n) a mass of burning material tied to a stick and carried to give light

brave (n) a young North American aboriginal warrior or fighting man

warrior (n) a soldier or experienced fighter

wigwam (n) a tent of the type used by some North American First Nations

huddled (v)	crowded close to someone or something
cheer her up (exp)	cause (somebody) to become happier or more cheerful
canoe (n)	a long, light, narrow boat, pointed at both ends, and moved by a paddle held in the hands
rushes (n)	grasslike water plants whose long thin hollow stems are often dried and made into mats and baskets
trembling (adj)	shaking uncontrollably, usually from fear or anxiety
crooning (v)	singing gently in a low soft voice
lodge (n)	a small house
vanished (v)	disappeared from sight
seized (v)	took hold of eagerly and forcefully
unbearable (adj)	not bearable; too bad to be borne
basked (v)	sat or lay in enjoyable heat or light

There may be other words and expressions in the story that are not familiar to you. Write each one in your journal. Then look it up in a dictionary, ask another student, or ask the teacher for a definition. Write the definition on the line beside the word or expression. Try to use the new word or expression in a sentence.

READING ACTIVITY

Make Connections

Scan the text and find the noun or nouns that the italicized pronoun refers to. The noun or nouns may be in the same sentence or somewhere else in the text. Write the answers in your journal and discuss them with the teacher and other students.

> EXAMPLE: *He* was the son of the West Wind and could do many wonderful things.
>
> ANSWER: *He* is Nanabozho.

1. *It* frightened the people and they would not keep it even for a day.
2. *She* saw the small trembling animal and picked it up.
3. He decided that *she* needed fire to warm her and cook her food.
4. *They* glowed with beautiful fiery colors.

5. After hiding his canoe in the rushes, *he* wondered how he could enter the wigwam and steal the torch.

6. *It* caught fire and the wind carried the flames and smoke back towards the girl.

7. *He* yawned and went back to sleep.

8. *They* ordered a young brave to take it to an old warrior who lived far away and would watch over it.

LISTENING ACTIVITY

Algonquian Legends

Look at the following list of traditional Algonquian activities. First, listen to the text. Second, listen to the text and indicate in your journal whether the activities were done by men, women, or both men and women. Third, listen to the text and complete the activity. Discuss the answers with the teacher and other students.

1. hunting
2. farming
3. fishing
4. travelling
5. making canoes
6. gathering food
7. living in wigwams
8. caring for children
9. fighting
10. making tools

DISCUSSION AND WRITING ACTIVITIES

My Favourite Grandparent

Choose one or more of your own grandparents, or choose a grandparent in a story or a movie. Identify and describe the person so that your listeners or readers have a clear idea of the person and his or her life. Share your stories with the teacher and other students. Which story is the most interesting, in your opinion? Why?

If I could be an animal, I'd be...

Imagine that you could change yourself into any animal at all. Of course, you could change back into yourself anytime you wished. Which animal would you like to be? Why? Mention at least three of the animal's qualities that you can identify with. Share your stories and decide who has told or written the most unusual one.

If I could be a tree, I'd be...

Imagine that you could change yourself into any type of tree at all. Of course, you could change back into yourself anytime you wished. Which type of tree would you like to be? Why? Mention at least three of the tree's qualities that you can identify with. Share your stories and decide who has told or written the most convincing one.

Fire!

The following are four sets of words and expressions related to fire. Choose one set of five words and create your own story about fire. Talk or write about it with the teacher and other students.

1. set on fire, fire alarm, fire department, fire engine, firefighter
2. light a fire, fireplace, firewood, fireguard, fireside
3. firecracker, on fire, fire station, firefighter, fire hydrant
4. firing squad, fire a gun, firearm, under fire, fire escape

Create a Legend

Make up a topic suitable for the creation of a legend. Here are some examples:

- where day and night came from
- where the four seasons came from
- where water came from
- where air came from
- where earth came from
- where fish came from
- where birds came from
- where people came from

Discuss these ideas with other students and then write a first draft of the legend. Illustrate it with sketches, if you wish.

Now read your legend to a group or the class. They may offer suggestions to make the legend and/or the illustrations more interesting. Then correct and complete the first draft of the legend and write a final draft.

First Nations Farmers of Eastern Canada

Choose one of these First Nations groups of Eastern Woodlands Farmers: (1) Cayuga, (2) Erie, (3) Huron, (4) Mohawk, (5) Oneida, (6) Onondaga, (7) Petun, and (8) Seneca.

Find out some information about the group, such as its history, territory, language, food, shelter, clothing, transportation, social and political organization, religion, art and leisure, or contemporary life.

Talk or write about the First Nations people that you have researched. In your opinion, what is the most interesting aspect of their culture?

LIBRARY BOOKS

If you would like to read other works by William Toye, look for the following books in the class, school, or local library, or in a bookstore.

The Fire Stealer
(Toronto: Oxford, 1979)
This edition is illustrated by Elizabeth Cleaver.

The Loon's Necklace
(Toronto: Oxford, 1977)
The retelling of a Tsimshian legend. Illustrated by Elizabeth Cleaver.

The Mountain Goats of Temlaham
(Toronto: Oxford, 1969)
Illustrated by Elizabeth Cleaver.

Cartier Discovers the St. Lawrence
(Toronto: Oxford, 1970)
A book for young people about the early French explorer Jacques Cartier. Illustrated by Laszlo Gal.

If you would like to read about Algonquan people and their legends, look for the following books in the class, school, or local library, or in a bookstore.

Tales from the Wigwam
(Toronto: Fitzhenry & Whiteside, 1989)
A collection of traditional tales adapted for young people.

Algonkian Hunters of the Eastern Woodlands
Claudine Goller
(Toronto: Grolier, 1984)
An illustrated book written for young people.

Algonkians of the Eastern Woodlands
Edward Rodgers
(Toronto: Royal Ontario Museum, 1990)
An illustrated book written for young people.

CHAPTER TEN

Roses Sing on New Snow
A Delicious Tale

by PAUL YEE

Dan Hobbs

WARM-UP

This is a story about a young Chinese Canadian woman named Maylin. She works in a restaurant in Chinatown. She is a wonderful cook. She might make a Chinese dish like this one.

Brainstorming

Brainstorming means that each and every person is able to contribute an idea to a topic of conversation. For example, each student in the class who has a response to any of the following questions should offer it to the whole class. Then discuss the responses together.

Have you ever worked or have you ever known anyone who worked in a restaurant? Tell the class about it. What was the job like? What was the schedule like? What was the salary like? What was the best part of the job? What was the worst part of the job? What is your opinion of working in a restaurant?

Have you ever eaten or have you ever known anyone who has eaten in a Chinese restaurant? Tell the class about it. What was it like? What was the food like? What are the names of some Chinese dishes? What is your opinion of Chinese food?

Introduction to the Story

Think about these questions as you read the story: What was Maylin's job in the Chinese restaurant? When did she work? How much did she get paid? What is "Roses Sing on New Snow"? You will discover the answers to these questions as you read the story.

$\mathscr{R}$oses Sing on New Snow

Seven days a week, every week of the year, Maylin cooked in her father's restaurant. It was a spot well known throughout the New World° for its fine food.

But when compliments and tips were sent to the chef, they never reached Maylin because her father kept the kitchen door closed and told everyone that it was his two sons who did all the cooking.

Maylin's father and brothers were fat and lazy from overeating, for they loved food.

Maylin loved food too, but for different reasons. To Chinatown came men lonely and cold and bone-tired°. Their families and wives waited in China.

But a well-cooked meal would always make them smile. So Maylin worked to renew their spirits and used only the best ingredients in her cooking.

Then one day it was announced that the governor of South China was coming to town. For a special banquet°, each restaurant in Chinatown was invited to bring its best dish.

Maylin's father ordered her to spare no expense° and to use all her imagination on a new dish. She shopped in the market for fresh fish and knelt in her garden for herbs and greens°.

In no time° she had fashioned a dish of delectable° flavors and aromas, which she named Roses Sing on New Snow.

Maylin's father sniffed happily and went off to the banquet, dressed in his best clothes and followed by his two sons.

Now the governor also loved to eat. His eyes lit up like lanterns at the array° of platters that arrived. Every kind of meat, every color of vegetable, every bouquet of spices was present. His chopsticks° dipped eagerly into every dish.

When he was done, he pointed to Maylin's bowl and said, "That one wins my warmest praise! It reminded me of China, and yet it transported me far beyond. Tell me, who cooked it?"

Maylin's father waddled° forward and repeated the lie he had told so often before. "Your Highness, it was my two sons who prepared it."

"Is that so?" The governor stroked his beard thoughtfully. "Then show my cook how the dish is done. I will present it to my emperor in China and reward you well!"

Maylin's father and brothers rushed home. They burst into the kitchen and forced Maylin to list all her ingredients. Then they made her demonstrate how she had chopped the fish and carved the vegetables and blended the spices.

They piled everything into huge baskets and then hurried back.

A stove was set up before the governor and his cook. Maylin's brothers cut the fish and cleaned the vegetables and ground the spices. They stoked a fire and cooked the food. But with one taste, the governor threw down his chopsticks.

"You imposters°! Do you take me for a fool?" he bellowed. "That is not Roses Sing on New Snow!"

Maylin's father tiptoed up and peeked. "Why...why, there is one spice not here," he stuttered°.

"Name it and I will send for it!" roared the impatient governor.

But Maylin's father had no reply, for he knew nothing about spices.

Maylin's older brother took a quick taste and said, "Why, there's one vegetable missing!"

"Name it, and my men will fetch° it!" ordered the governor.

But no reply came, for Maylin's older brother knew nothing about food.

Maylin's other brother blamed the fishmonger°. "He gave us the wrong kind of fish!" he cried.

"Then name the right one, and my men will fetch it!" said the governor.

Again there was no answer.

Maylin's father and brothers quaked with fear and fell to their knees. When the governor pounded his fist on the chair, the truth quickly spilled out. The guests were astounded° to hear that a woman had cooked this dish. Maylin's father hung his head in shame° as the governor sent for the real cook.

Maylin strode in and faced the governor and his men. "Your Excellency, you cannot take this dish to China!" she announced.

"What?" cried the governor. "You dare refuse the emperor a chance to taste this wonderful creation?"

"This is a dish of the New World," Maylin said. "You cannot recreate it in the Old."

But the governor ignored her words and scowled°. "I can make your father's life miserable here," he threatened her. So she said, "Let you and I cook side by side°, so you can see for yourself."

The guests gasped° at her daring request. However, the governor nodded, rolled up his sleeves, and donned° an apron. Together, Maylin and the governor cut and chopped. Side by side they heated two woks°, and then stirred in identical ingredients.

When the two dishes were finally finished, the governor took a taste from both. His face paled, for they were different.

"What is your secret?" he demanded. "We selected the same ingredients and cooked side by side!"

"If you and I sat down with paper and brush and black ink, could we bring forth identical paintings?" asked Maylin.

From that day on Maylin was renowned in Chinatown as a great cook and a wise person. Her fame even reached as far as China.

But the emperor, despite the governor's best efforts, was never able to taste that most delicious New World dish, nor to hear Roses Sing on New Snow.

GLOSSARY

New World (n)	North, Central, or South America; the Western Hemisphere
bone-tired (adj)	extremely tired or in great need of rest and sleep
banquet (n)	a formal dinner for many people in honour of a special person or occasion, especially one at which speeches are made
spare no expense (exp)	spend a lot of money
greens (n)	green leafy vegetables that are cooked and eaten
in no time (exp)	very quickly
delectable (adj)	very pleasing; delightful
array (n)	a fine show, collection, or ordered group

chopsticks (n)	a pair of narrow sticks held between the thumb and fingers and used in East Asian countries when eating food
waddled (v)	walked with short steps, moving one's body from one side to the other, like a duck
imposters (n)	people who deceive by pretending to be other people
stuttered (v)	spoke with difficulty in producing sounds, especially the first sound of a word
fetch (v)	go and get and bring back
fishmonger (n)	someone who works in a shop that sells fish
astounded (adj)	very much surprised
in shame (exp)	with the painful feeling of one's own guilt, wrongness, or failure; in disgrace; in dishonour
scowled (v)	made an angry, threatening expression of the face
side by side (exp)	next to one another
gasped (v)	caught the breath suddenly, especially because of surprise or shock
donned (v)	put on (clothes)
woks (n)	bowls used in East Asian countries for cooking food over heat

There may be other words and expressions in the story that are not familiar to you. Write each one in your journal. Then look it up in a dictionary, ask another student, or ask the teacher for a definition. Write the definition on the line beside the word or expression. Try to use the new word or expression in a sentence.

READING ACTIVITY

Correct the Information

This is a summary of the story, but there are some mistakes in it. Write the mistaken words in your journal and beside them write correct ones. Discuss the answers with the teacher and other students.

Summary

This is a short story about an old woman named Maylin. She worked in her father's flower store. Her father would tell his customers that his three daughters did all the work. The customers made a dish called Roses Sing on New Snow. The dish was given to the emperor of South China. He asked who painted it. He was told that Maylin's two sisters did the work. The emperor wanted to know how to make the dish. Maylin's brothers tried to make Roses Sing on New Snow, but it didn't smell the same. The emperor became angry. Maylin's uncle told the governor that Maylin made the dish. Maylin showed the governor how to make Roses Sing on New Snow, but he wasn't able to make it look the same. Only Maylin was able to paint Roses Sing on New Snow.

LISTENING ACTIVITY

Paul Yee

This is a text about the life of Paul Yee. First, listen to the text. Second, listen to the text and write as much of it as you can in your journal. Third, listen to the text and complete it. Then go over it with the teacher and other students.

DISCUSSION AND WRITING ACTIVITIES

Maylin's Recipe for Roses Sing on New Snow

Maylin made a delectable dish called Roses Sing on New Snow. She used these ingredients: (1) fish, (2) greens or vegetables, and (3) herbs and spices. Unfortunately, we don't know what kind of fish or greens or herbs and spices she used. And we don't know how she cooked the ingredients or how she arranged them on a plate.

Talk or write about the recipe for Roses Sing on New Snow. First, state the exact ingredients. Second, specify the exact quantity of the ingredients. Third, give the directions for making the dish. Share your recipe with the teacher and other students.

Your Favourite Recipe

Talk or write about your own favourite recipe. First, state the exact ingredients. Second, specify the exact quantity of the ingredients. Third, give the directions for making the dish. Share your recipe with the teacher and other students.

Words of Wisdom

Maylin made these two statements in the story:

1. "Your Excellency, you cannot take this dish to China!" she announced. "This is a dish of the New World. You cannot recreate it in the Old."
2. "If you and I sat down with paper and brush and black ink, could we bring forth identical paintings?" asked Maylin.

Do you agree or disagree with Maylin? Talk or write about one or both of these statements with the teacher and other students. Use your own knowledge and experience to support your opinions.

All Work and No Play

There is an English expression that says, "All work and no play makes Jack a dull boy." What do you think this expression means? Maylin worked seven days a week, every week of the year. She did not have a day off; nor did she have a vacation. What is your opinion of her work schedule? Talk or write about the arguments that you would use to make her work schedule more humane.

Daddy Dearest

Maylin did the cooking in her father's restaurant, but he did not give her the compliments or the tips that the customers sent to her. Her father and her two brothers were fat and lazy from eating too much. Her father lied to everyone and said that her two brothers did the cooking. Her father had to hang his head in shame when the governor forced him to tell the truth.

Talk or write about the way Maylin's father treats his daughter and the way he treats his sons. Do fathers usually treat their sons and daughters differently? Do mothers treat their sons and daughters differently, too? Do you think that families from different cultures treat sons and daughters differently? Do you think that they continue to do so today? How do you think boys and girls in the same family should be treated? Use your own knowledge and experience to support your opinions. Share them with the teacher and other students.

Restaurant Reviews

People came to eat in Maylin's father's restaurant because of the fine food. It renewed their spirits and made them smile.

Talk or write about the reasons why people go to restaurants. Mention the food, the prices, the service, the décor, the location, the opening and closing hours, the methods of payment, and special features such as access for wheelchairs, no smoking areas, music and dancing, and so on. Which features do you think are the most important? Why?

Name several restaurants in your area. Choose one of them and describe it in detail. Be sure to include your personal opinion of the restaurant, too, if you have eaten there. Share your review with the teacher and other students.

LIBRARY BOOKS

If you would like to read other works by Paul Yee, look for the following books in the class, school, or local library, or in a bookstore.

Roses Sing on New Snow
(Vancouver: Douglas & McIntyre, 1991)
This edition features illustrations by Harvey Chan.

Curses of the Third Uncle
(Toronto: Lorimer, 1986)
A young adult novel about a 14-year-old girl's fight to prevent her uncle from sending her family back to China. The action takes place in Vancouver's Chinatown in 1909.

Saltwater City
(Vancouver: Douglas & McIntyre, 1988)
An illustrated history of the Chinese in Vancouver.

Tales of the Gold Mountain
(Vancouver: Douglas & McIntyre, 1989)
Eight original stories of the Chinese in Canada. Written for young adults, with illustrations by Simon Ng.

Teach Me to Fly, Skyfighter! and Other Stories
(Toronto: Lorimer, 1983)
A young adult's book featuring four stories of contemporary life in Vancouver's Chinatown and Strathcona district. Illustrated by Sky Lee.

If you would like to read more about Chinese Canadians, look for the following books in the class, school, or local library, or in a bookstore.

In a Strange Land
Richard T. Wright
(Saskatoon: Western Producer Prairie, 1988)
A pictorial record of the first Chinese people in Canada, covering the years 1778 to 1823.

Many Mouthed Birds
Bennett Lee and Jim Wong-Chu, editors
(Vancouver: Douglas & McIntyre, 1991)
A collection of contemporary writing by Chinese Canadians, including a poem by Paul Yee.

A Taste of Chinatown
Joie Warner
(Toronto: Little, Brown, 1989)
A collection of Chinese recipes, with photographs by Drew Warner.

CHAPTER ELEVEN

The Poor Cottage

PHILIPPE-JOSEPH AUBERT DE GASPÉ
translated by Jane Brierly

National Archives of Canada (C–14256)

WARM-UP

Look at the picture carefully. This is Philippe-Joseph Aubert de Gaspé. He wrote
"The Poor Cottage" in 1863, but it is about people who lived in Normandy in
France before then. It is one tale in his book *Yellow-Wolf and other Tales of the
Saint Lawrence.*

Scanning for Specific Information

Sometimes we scan a piece of writing to find a few facts. We don't read everything.
We don't even need to get a general idea about the piece of writing. We need only
the specific pieces of information. We do this by reading very quickly.

In this activity, you will try to answer the following questions below by scanning the summary of the story below. Try to answer each question in ten seconds or less.

1. What does the family have for supper?
2. Where do they live?
3. How do they feel?
4. Who do they ask for help?
5. Who knocks on the door?
6. What does she want?
7. Who has a lot of food?
8. Who gave the old woman food and shelter?
9. What happens to the rich man?
10. What happens to the poor family?

Summary

This is a story about a very poor family. They do not have enough food to eat. In fact, they have only a quarter of a loaf of bread for supper, and the parents give some to their four younger children. The parents and their two older children sit by a small fire in their hut or small house. They are very cold and hungry and they pray to God to help them.

Suddenly an old woman knocks on the door. She is also very cold and hungry and asks the family to give her something to eat. They only have a little bit of bread, but they give it to her. She asks them for more, and the father says that he will go to his rich neighbour's house and ask for some. The old woman says that she has already gone there, and that the rich man refused to give her either food or shelter.

A terrible thunder and lightning storm begins. The old woman tells the family that God is angry at the rich man and will punish him, but that God will reward the poor family. They will always have bread in the bread box or hutch from now on.

Introduction to the Story

Tales such as these were told a long time ago so they contain words and expressions that were used a long time ago. This does not mean that you cannot read and enjoy these stories today. You simply have to pay special attention to those words and expressions.

Here are some words in "The Poor Cottage" that are rarely heard today:

wuthering (v)	blowing
fagot (n)	a bunch of small sticks for burning
hark (v)	listen
behest (n)	request
passeth (v)	the verb "passes"
nabob (n)	a very rich man
beldam (n)	from the French, *belle dame*, or gentle lady

Do you know any other words or expressions like these in English or in another language? What are they? What do they mean? Make a list of them and discuss them with the teacher and other students.

☞he Poor Cottage

There was once a family of poor peasants° consisting of father, mother, and six young children. They lived in a little thatched° cottage on the edge of a Normandy forest. Let us enter this miserable hut. It was eight o'clock in the evening on a dark November night. The wind had been wuthering and the rain falling in torrents for a week, as though the waterfalls of heaven had opened and were threatening Earth with a second Flood°. The parents and two of the children, aged ten and twelve, watched by the hearth° where a dwindling fagot burned, despite wind and water swirling down the chimney. Occasional puffs of smoke left the watchers in total darkness. The four youngest children lay sleeping on piles of filthy rags and straw°.

"What misery and heartache poor people have to bear before they die," said the woodcutter° sadly. "It makes me lose heart°!"

"You've never talked like this before, my man," said the woman. "Have you lost faith in God and Our Lady° — and you such a good Christian?"

"No indeed," replied the husband. "Without that faith to sustain° me, without my love for my family, I'd have died of heartbreak long ago. I've never complained about my suffering before God or man. It's your misery, dear wife and children, that tears at my heart. This evening there was only a quarter of a loaf of bread left in the hutch, and the four youngest wept with hunger. We gave each of them a small piece, and now they're asleep. But you — you're going without food to dry the tears of poor innocents too young to understand our poverty. It's enough to make a man tear his hair° in despair!"

There was a moment of silence within the hut, made more solemn by the raging elements outside and the sobs of mother and children. Then the woodcutter spoke.

"You're right, my dear wife, I've failed in my duty. This is the hour of prayer. Let us pray to the good Lord with fervour° and trust, and beg forgiveness for me in this moment of weakness."

This act of Christian piety° was barely done when a knock on the door startled the family. "Come in," said the peasant. The door of the hut opened to admit an aged woman bent double°, walking with the help of a long cane. The family hurried to help her off with a dripping old cape that barely covered her shoulders, then sat her down beside the hearth and threw another fagot on the fire.

"I'm hungry," said the beggar-woman, once she had warmed herself. "Give me some supper, for the love of God."

"We're very poor, my good mother°," replied the peasant. "We've nothing but bread, but I offer you that with all my heart." And so saying, he gave her the little bit of bread that remained in the hutch. While the old woman devoured this meagre fare°, the children gazed at her tearfully.

"I've had nothing to eat for two days," said the old woman, once she had downed the last mouthful. "Another bit of bread for the love of Our Lady!"

"We have no more," said the woodcutter. "But wait, good mother — I'll run over to my neighbour's house not half a league° from here. He's rich and has plenty of everything. He knows I'm honest and hardworking, and he won't refuse me a loaf of bread."

"He'll be poorer than you tomorrow," said the old woman with assurance°. "I've just come from his house, and not only did he refuse me the shelter of his roof this terrible night: he even denied me the paltry scrap of bread one gives to the poor. But hark!"

The raging wind fell silent as if at the behest of some powerful genie, and a bright fire blazed up on the hearth. The beating of wings was heard, as though a huge bird with a twenty-foot wingspan had passed over the forest.

"It's the ministering angel of God's justice," said the old woman solemnly, "going his nocturnal round in the kingdom of Saint Louis°, the friend and father of the poor on earth and in heaven!"

The family was seized with terror at this pronouncement°, and all fell face down on the earthen floor. The old woman rose from her seat, opened the door of the hut, and stretched her hand toward the dwelling of the pitiless rich man. "Behold the justice of the Lord passeth over!" she cried. An immense bolt of lightning lit up the sky and a dreadful clap of thunder shook the forest as torrents of flame heralded the merciless nabob's ruin.

"Have pity! Have pity on him!" cried the woodcutter and his wife.

"The justice of the Almighty is inflexible°," replied the old woman with authority. "This man has always refused the poor the shelter of his roof and the crumbs from his table. The hand of God has struck justly!" The beldam said nothing for a moment, then added, "The hutch from which you took the last bit of bread for the poor beggar-woman will fill up as fast as you can empty it, and when you are rich, you will build a shelter for suffering humanity in place of this hovel." And with these words she disappeared.

GLOSSARY

peasants (n)	(used in former times) a person who works on the land, especially one who owns and lives on a small piece of land
thatched (adj)	with a roof covering made of straw or reeds
Flood (n)	a flood is the covering with water of a place that is usually dry or a great overflow of water; the Flood refers to the story in the Bible of Noah and the Ark
hearth (n)	the area around the fire in one's home, especially the floor of the fireplace
straw (n)	dried stems of grain plants, such as wheat, used for animals to sleep on
woodcutter (n)	a person whose job is to cut down trees
lose heart (exp)	lose courage or firmness of purpose
Our Lady (n)	a name for Mary, the mother of Jesus
sustain (v)	keep strong; strengthen
tear his hair (exp)	feel hopeless
fervour (n)	showing strong and warm feelings
piety (n)	deep respect for God and religion
bent double (exp)	sloped or leaned away from an upright position
good mother (exp)	an older woman who is kind and loving
meagre fare (n)	not enough food, especially for a meal

half a league (n)	an old unit of measurement, equal to about two or three kilometres
assurance (n)	certainty; confidence
Saint Louis (n)	Louis XI, a king of France who devoted his life to helping the poor
pronouncement (n)	a solemn declaration or statement
inflexible (adj)	cannot be bent or turned away from a purpose

There may be other words and expressions in the story that are not familiar to you. Write each one in your journal. Then look it up in a dictionary, ask another student, or ask the teacher for a definition. Write the definition on the line beside the word or expression. Try to use the new word or expression in a sentence.

READING ACTIVITY

Guess the Meaning of Words from Context

Match each italicized word in the sentences with one of the meanings in the list below. Sometimes, you will be able to guess the meaning of the word from the sentence (from the context); other times, you will have to read what comes before and after that sentence in the text.

1. The rain fell in *torrents* for a week.
2. A *dwindling* log burned in the fireplace.
3. The children lay on piles of *filthy* rags.
4. What *misery* and heartache poor people have to bear!
5. A knock on the door *startled* the family.
6. The old woman was so hungry she *devoured* the bread.
7. The rich man did not give her a *paltry scrap* of bread.
8. The raging wind fell silent as if some *genie* had power over it.
9. The angel is going on his *nocturnal* round.
10. You will build a shelter for people in place of this *hovel*.

a) active at night
b) ate up quickly

c) becoming gradually smaller or fewer

d) caused to jump with sudden surprise

e) great unhappiness or great pain and suffering

f) magical spirit in Arab fairy stories

g) small dirty place to live in

h) very dirty

i) violently rushing streams of water

j) worthless or very small piece (of food)

LISTENING ACTIVITY

Philippe-Joseph Aubert de Gaspé

This is a summary of important dates in the life of Philippe-Joseph Aubert de Gaspé. First, listen to the text. Second, listen to the text and fill in the blanks in your journal. Third, listen to the text and complete the blanks. Discuss the answers with the teacher and other students.

1786	Philippe-Joseph Aubert de Gaspé was born in Quebec City.
1790s – early 1800s	_____
_____	He was the sheriff of Quebec City.
1837	_____
_____	He published his first book, *Les Ançiens canadiens*.
1866	_____
_____	He died in Quebec City.

DISCUSSION AND WRITING ACTIVITIES

Point of View

The story is told from the point of view of the woodcutter. Retell the story, either orally or in writing, from the point of view of (1) the woodcutter's wife, (2) the two older children, (3) the old woman, or (4) the rich man.

A Dark and Stormy Night

Create and develop your own story, beginning with the famous first line, "It was a dark and stormy night." Share your story with the teacher and other students. Whose story was the most suspenseful? Why?

Canadian Women of Long Ago

The women listed below helped people in Canada a long time ago. Choose one of them and find out some information about her and the times in which she lived. Then talk or write about your information with other students.

Jeanne Mance

Marguerite Bourgeoys

Marie de l'Incarnation

Marie Marguerite d'Youville

Mother Marie-Léonie

Mother Marie-Rose

Canadian Men of Long Ago

The men listed below helped people to settle in Canada a long time ago. Choose one of them and find out some information about him and the times in which he lived. Then talk or write about your information with other students.

François de Laval

Jacques Cartier

Jacques Marquette

Jean de Brébeuf

Louis Hébert

Samuel de Champlain

Bread

Brainstorm about the topic of bread. Name different types of bread. Which ones do you like or dislike? Why? Do you buy bread? Where? How much does it cost? Do you make bread? Why? What is your recipe? What is your favourite recipe that contains bread as an ingredient?

Poverty

According to economics, poverty is defined as the inability of people to provide the necessities of life. However, poverty is not simply an economic matter. How much stress and helplessness must people suffer before they are considered poor? Find out some information about poverty in Canada: Who are the poor? What is the poverty line? What are anti-poverty programs and what effect do they have on people?

LIBRARY BOOKS

If you would like to read other works by Philippe-Joseph Aubert de Gaspé, look for the following books in the class, school, or local library, or in a bookstore.

Yellow-Wolf and Other Tales of the Saint Lawrence
(Montreal: Véhicule, 1990)
A collection of stories and memoirs from which "The Poor Cottage" was taken. This edition was translated by Jane Brierly.

Canadians of Old
(Toronto: McClelland & Stewart, 1974)
A historical novel set in the 18th-century, first published as *Les Anciens canadiens* in 1863. This edition was translated by Sir Charles G. D. Roberts and first published in 1890.

A Man of Sentiment
(Montreal: Véhicule, 1988)
A collection of tales and memories of early 19th-century French Canadian life. First published in French in 1866 as *Mémoires*. This edition was translated by Jane Brierley.

If you would like to read more about the times Philippe-Joseph Aubert de Gaspé wrote about, look for the following books in the class, school, or local library, or in a bookstore.

Folklore of Canada
Edith Fowke
(Toronto: McClelland & Stewart, 1982)
A collection of folk tales, legends, and other kinds of folklore from all regions of Canada.

New France
Rosemary Livesey
(Toronto: Stoddart, 1989)
An illustrated look at the people of New France, and how they lived.

CHAPTER TWELVE

Water Poetry

HECTOR DE SAINT-DENYS GARNEAU, F. R. SCOTT, and RAYMOND SOUSTER

John McNeill

WARM-UP

Look at the picture carefully. What do you see in it? How does it make you think and feel? If you wrote a poem about this picture, what would you write? Why? Many well-known Canadian poets have written poems about water. One of them is Hector de Saint-Denys Garneau.

Listening Activity

This is a text on the life of Hector de Saint-Denys Garneau. First, listen to the text. Second, listen to the text and write as much of it as you can in your journal.

Third, listen to the text and complete it. Discuss it with the teacher and other students.

Introduction to the Poems

There are three poems in this chapter. They are all about water. If you wrote a poem about water, what would you write about: a stream? a river? a pool? a pond? a lake? the sea? the ocean? Why? What do you think these poets wrote about? Listen to the poems and read them as many times as you wish.

oems

Poem 1

Ice mothers me
My bed is rock
Over sand I move silently.

I am crystal clear
To a sunbeam°.
No grasses grow in me
My banks° are clean.

Foam runs from the rapid
To rest on my dark pools.

Poem 2

O my eyes this morning, wide as a river
O wave of my eyes swift to reflect all things
And this coolness under my eyelids
A marvel
Circling the images I see

As a stream cools an island
And as the fluent wave curls around
That sun-dappled° girl

Poem 3

No-one knows the exact moment
of what hour
the first drop of rain will fall.

But after one whole week
of blinding sun
of scorched° grass
of wilting° leaves,
it somehow seems important.

So I watch and wait
along with the birds,
along with the ants,
along with every living
breathing thing,

for that first heavy
cool splash of rain
to wet the page
of this poem about the rain.

GLOSSARY

sunbeam (n)	a ray or line of natural light from the sun
banks (n)	the land or shore along the sides of a river or a lake
sun-dappled (adj)	marked with spots of sun and shadow
scorched (adj)	burned so as to change a thing's colour, taste, or feeling, but not to destroy it completely
wilting (adj)	becoming less fresh and starting to die

There may be other words and expressions in the poems that are not familiar to you. Write each one in your journal. Then look it up in a dictionary, ask another student, or ask the teacher for a definition. Write the definition on the line beside the word or expression. Try to use the new word or expression in a sentence.

READING ACTIVITIES

Mix and Match

Read the three poems again. In pairs or small groups, decide what title you would give to each poem. Write your choices in your journal and discuss the reasons for them with the teacher and other students.

Poem 1

Poem 2

Poem 3

Read the poems again and match them with the actual titles in your journal. Discuss your choices and the reasons for them with the teacher and other students.

Poem 1   a) "Waiting for the First Drop"

Poem 2   b) "North Stream"

Poem 3   c) "River of My Eyes"

Analyze the Poems

Discuss the answers to these questions with the teacher and other students:

1. Who is the speaker in each poem?
2. What kind of person does he or she seem to be?
3. To whom is he or she speaking?
4. What is the speaker's point of view and relation to the subject?
5. What is the general mood or feeling (tone) of each poem?
6. Is the feeling consistent from poem to poem or is there a shift in tone?
7. What is the situation or occasion of each poem?
8. What is the setting in time and space of each poem?

LISTENING ACTIVITY

Interactive Dictation

An interactive dictation is similar to a dictation, such as the one in the warm-up, but the texts are dictated by students to students.

An interactive dictation is done in pairs. One member of the pair is Student A and the other member is Student B. Student A is the only one who looks at the text marked Student A, and Student B is the only one who looks at the text marked Student B.

Student A takes the first turn. Student A dictates a text on the life of F. R. Scott to Student B. That is, Student A will read the text first, read the text with pauses a second time, and then read the text a third time.

Student B takes the second turn. Student B dictates a text on the life of Raymond Souster to Student A. That is, Student B will read the text three times, following the procedure described for Student A.

In order to correct the interactive dictation, Student A looks at Student B's journal, and Student B looks at Student A's journal. Discuss the corrections with the teacher and other students.

STUDENT A

Read to Student B

Francis Reginald Scott was born in Quebec City in 1899. His father, F. G. Scott, was an Anglican minister and a poet. F. R. Scott studied law at McGill University in Montreal and Oxford University in England. After he returned to Canada, Scott worked as a lawyer and taught at McGill. He also became involved in politics and was one of the leading members of the New Democratic Party. Much of F. R. Scott's poetry deals with social issues. A great many other poems demonstrate his love of Canadian landscapes and water-scapes. F. R. Scott died in Montreal in 1985.

Write in Your Journal

Raymond Souster

STUDENT B

Read to Student A

Raymond Souster was born in 1921 in Toronto. He has lived in Toronto nearly all his life and worked for more than 45 years in a bank there. His first book of poems, *When We Were Young*, was published in 1946. His most famous book is *The Colour of the Times*, which won the Governor General's Award for poetry in 1964. Some of Souster's better collections include *A Local Pride* and *As Is*.

Write in Your Journal

F. R. Scott

DISCUSSION AND WRITING ACTIVITIES

Match the Poems and the Poets

Read the poems again and match them with the actual authors in your journal. Discuss your choices and the reasons for them with the teacher and other students.

Poem 1   a) Hector de Saint-Denys Garneau translated by John Glassco
Poem 2   b) Raymond Souster
Poem 3   c) F. R. Scott

Evaluate the Poets

Talk or write about your evaluation of each poet. Do you like each poet's work? If so, why? If not, why not? How does the work of these poets compare to the work of your own favourite poets?

Identify "Poetic License"

"Poetic license" allows poetry to depart from the standard rules of logic and grammar. If you are not sure what "poetic license" is, discuss it with the teacher and other students. Then talk or write about the "poetic license" in the poems above. Give other examples of "poetic license" from the poetry you have read.

Describe the Symbols and Images

Talk or write about the symbols, images, and figures of speech in the poems above. Compare and contrast the symbols, images, and figures of speech in at least two of the poems. Give other examples of symbols, images, and figures of speech from the poetry you have read.

Describe the Rhyme and Metre

Talk or write about the rhyme and metre in the poems above. Compare and contrast the rhyme and metre in at least two of the poems. Give other examples of rhyme and metre from the poetry you have read.

Talk or write about your evaluation of each poem. What is your reaction to each poem? Do you like each poem? If so, why? If not, why not? How do the poems compare to your own favourite poems?

LIBRARY BOOKS

If you would like to read other poems by Hector de Saint-Denys Garneau, F. R. Scott, and Raymond Souster, look for the following books in the class, school, or local library, or in a bookstore.

The Complete Poems of Saint-Denys Garneau
(Ottawa: Oberon, 1975)
Garneau's collected poems, first published in French in 1949 as *Poésies complètes*. This translation is by John Glassco.

The Collected Poems of F. R. Scott
(Toronto: McClelland & Stewart, 1981)
The winner of the 1981 Governor General's Award for poetry. This book contains French Canadian poems translated by Scott, including some by Hector de Saint-Denys Garneau.

The Colour of the Times
(Toronto: Ryerson, 1964)
A collection of Souster's poems up to 1964. Winner of the Governor General's Award for poetry.

Jubilee of Death
(Ottawa: Oberon, 1984)
Poems by Souster concerning the Dieppe Raid in World War II, a disastrous military campaign in which 907 Canadian soldiers died.

If you would like to read more about the lives and works of Hector de Saint-Denys Garneau, F. R. Scott, and Raymond Souster, look for the following books in the class, school, or local library, or in a bookstore.

The Journal of Saint-Denys Garneau
(Toronto: McClelland & Stewart, 1962)
A journal kept by the poet between 1935 and 1939, first published in French in 1954 as *Journal*. This translation is by John Glassco.

The Politics of the Imagination
Sandra Djwa
(Toronto: McClelland & Stewart, 1987)
The major biography of F. R. Scott.

Raymond Souster and His Works
Bruce Whiteman
(Toronto: ECW, 1984)
A brief book of biography and criticism.

CHAPTER THIRTEEN

My Financial Career

STEPHEN LEACOCK

Fort Frances Canadian Imperial Bank of Commerce; ACCP. 6693, S11390; Archives of Ontario

WARM-UP

Stephen Leacock was a teacher and an economist, but he is most famous for his books of humour. He was one of the first Canadian writers to earn worldwide popularity, and his books have been published in 18 languages.

Brainstorming

Brainstorming means that each and every person is able to contribute an idea to a topic of conversation. For example, each student in the class who has a response to any of the questions below should offer it to the whole class. Then discuss the responses together.

What are some of the services offered by banks? Have you ever done business, or have you ever known anyone who has transacted business, with a bank or financial institution? Tell the class about it. What was it like? What were the people like? How did the customer feel about the services offered by the bank or financial institution?

Have you ever worked or have you ever known anyone who has worked in a bank or financial institution? Tell the class about it. What was the job like? What was the schedule like? What was the salary like? What was the best part of the job? What was the worst part of the job? What is your opinion of working in a bank or financial institution?

Introduction to the Story

Think about these questions as you read the story: What does the narrator want to do in the bank? Why? How does he feel about it? What happens? How is he treated by the people who work in the bank? You will discover the answers to these questions as you read the story.

My Financial Career

When I go into a bank I get rattled°. The clerks rattle me; the wickets° rattle me; the sight of the money rattles me; everything rattles me.

The moment I cross the threshold° of a bank and attempt to transact business there, I become an irresponsible idiot.

I knew this beforehand, but my salary had been raised to fifty dollars a month and I felt that the bank was the only place for it.

So I shambled° in and looked timidly round at the clerks. I had an idea that a person about to open an account must needs° consult the manager.

I went up to a wicket marked "Accountant." The accountant was a tall, cool devil°. The very sight of him rattled me. My voice was sepulchral°.

"Can I see the manager?" I said, and added solemnly, "alone." I don't know why I said "alone."

"Certainly," said the accountant, and fetched him.

The manager was a grave, calm man. I held my fifty-six dollars clutched in a crumpled ball in my pocket.

"Are you the manager?" I said. God knows I didn't doubt it.

"Yes," he said.

"Can I see you," I asked, "alone?" I didn't want to say "alone" again, but without it the thing seemed self-evident.

The manager looked at me in some alarm. He felt that I had an awful secret to reveal.

"Come in here," he said, and led the way to a private room. He turned the key in the lock.

"We are safe from interruption here," he said; "sit down."

We both sat down and looked at each other. I found no voice to speak.

"You are one of Pinkerton's° men, I presume," he said.

He had gathered from my mysterious manner that I was a detective. I knew what he was thinking, and it made me worse.

"No, not from Pinkerton's," I said, seeming to imply that I came from a rival agency.

"To tell the truth," I went on, as if I had been prompted to lie about it, "I am not a detective at all. I have come to open an account. I intend to keep all my money in this bank."

The manager looked relieved but still serious; he concluded now that I was a son of Baron Rothschild° or a young Gould°.

"A large account, I suppose," he said.

"Fairly large," I whispered. "I propose to deposit fifty-six dollars now and fifty dollars a month regularly."

The manager got up and opened the door. He called to the accountant.

"Mr. Montgomery," he said unkindly loud, "this gentleman is opening an account; he will deposit fifty-six dollars. Good morning."

I rose.

A big iron door stood open at the side of the room.

"Good morning," I said, and stepped into the safe°.

"Come out," said the manager coldly, and showed me the other way.

I went up to the accountant's wicket and poked the ball of money at him with a quick convulsive movement as if I were doing a conjuring° trick.

My face was ghastly° pale.

"Here," I said, "deposit it." The tone of the words seemed to mean, "Let us do this painful thing while the fit° is on us."

He took the money and gave it to another clerk.

He made me write the sum on a slip and sign my name in a book. I no longer knew what I was doing. The bank swam before my eyes.

"Is it deposited?" I asked in a hollow, vibrating voice.

"It is," said the accountant.

"Then I want to draw a cheque."

My idea was to draw out six dollars of it for present use. Someone gave me a cheque-book through a wicket and someone else began telling me how to write it out. The people in the bank had the impression that I was an invalid ° millionaire. I wrote something on the cheque and thrust it in at the clerk. He looked at it.

"What! are you drawing it all out again?" he asked in surprise. Then I realized that I had written fifty-six instead of six. I was too far gone° to reason now. I had a feeling that it was impossible to explain the thing. All the clerks had stopped writing to look at me.

Reckless with misery, I made a plunge°.

"Yes, the whole thing."

"You withdraw your money from the bank?"

"Every cent of it.".

"Are you not going to deposit any more?" said the clerk, astonished.

"Never."

An idiot hope struck me that they might think something had insulted me while I was writing the cheque and that I had changed my mind°. I made a wretched attempt to look like a man with a fearfully quick temper°.

The clerk prepared to pay the money.

"How will you have it?" he said.

"What?"

"How will you have it?"

"Oh" — I caught his meaning and answered without even thinking — "in fifties."

He gave me a fifty-dollar bill.

"And the six?" he asked dryly.

"In sixes," I said.

He gave it to me and I rushed out.

As the big door swung behind me I caught the echo of a roar of laughter that went up to the ceiling of the bank. Since then I bank no more. I keep my money in cash in my trousers pocket and keep my savings in silver dollars° in a sock.

GLOSSARY

rattled (v)	made nervous or anxious
wickets (n)	enclosures or cages, sometimes with bars
threshold (n)	a piece of wood or stone fixed beneath the door into a house or building

shambled (v)	walked in slowly
must needs (exp)	colloquial English; the standard English would be either "must" or "needs to"
devil (n)	(in expressions of strong feeling) fellow, man, or boy
sepulchral (adj)	sombre like a burial place or a tomb
Pinkerton's (n)	a private detective agency founded in the United States and now operating security services internationally
Baron Rothschild	head of a famous international banking family whose fortunes developed in Europe during the Napoleonic Wars
Gould	early American capitalist whose wealth came through control of railroads
safe (n)	a cupboard or small room with thick metal sides and a lock, used for protecting money and valuables from thieves
conjuring (adj)	causing to appear by or as if by magic
ghastly (adj)	very white and ill-looking
fit (n)	a short attack of a slight illness or violent feeling
invalid (adj)	made weak by illness
too far gone (exp)	too confused or upset to think clearly
plunge (n)	decision to perform an act determinedly, after having delayed through anxiety or uncertainty
changed my mind (exp)	changed one's intentions or opinions
quick temper (exp)	an angry state of mind
silver dollars (n)	dollars in the form of silver coins

There may be other words and expressions in the story that are not familiar to you. Write each one in your journal. Then look it up in a dictionary, ask another student, or ask the teacher for a definition. Write the definition on the line beside the word or expression. Try to use the new word or expression in a sentence.

READING ACTIVITIES

Inference Questions

Sometimes you can find information in a text that is not stated clearly in the words. You infer the information — that is, you make a logical guess — from either what is in the text, or your knowledge of the world, or both.

Try to infer the probable answers to the questions below by looking at the text. Be ready to give your reasons. Discuss the answers with the teacher and other students.

1. Is the manager happy when he receives visits from Pinkerton's men?
2. Is the son of Baron Rothschild a rich man?
3. Does the bank manager think that $56 is a lot of money?
4. Does the manager usually meet with people who are opening accounts?
5. Do the people in the bank feel sorry that the narrator isn't keeping his money with them?

Attitudes and Feelings

Here is a list of adjectives used in the story. Choose the correct word to describe each person in the story: the narrator, the clerk, the manager, and the accountant. Be careful: there are some extra adjectives. Discuss the answers with the teacher and other students.

1. astonished
2. cool
3. grave
4. disappointed
5. worried
6. rattled
7. solemn
8. unkind

LISTENING ACTIVITY

Stephen Leacock

This is a text about the life of Stephen Leacock. First, listen to the text. Second, listen to the text and answer each question below in your journal. Third, listen to the text and check your answers. Discuss the answers with the teacher and other students.

1. Where and when was Stephen Leacock born?
2. When did his family emigrate to Canada?
3. Where did they settle?
4. Where did Stephen Leacock study?
5. Where did he work in 1903?
6. What was the name of his first book?
7. When was it published?
8. What was the name of his first book of humour?
9. When was it published?
10. When did Stephen Leacock retire?
11. When did Stephen Leacock die?
12. When was the Stephen Leacock Medal for Humour created?

DISCUSSION AND WRITING ACTIVITIES

My Most Embarrassing Moment

Talk or write about your most embarrassing moment. Describe the incident in detail so that your listeners or readers know exactly what happened to you.

A Step-by-Step Process

Choose a sequential process or situation, such as these:

- opening a savings account
- closing a savings account
- depositing money in the bank
- withdrawing money from the bank
- starting a car
- making a cake
- planting a tree

Talk or write about the step-by-step process with the teacher and other students.

Banks

Talk or write about two different banks or financial institutions. Compare and contrast the services that they offer to their customers. Which bank would you choose to go to? Why?

Money in the Mattress

Some people put all their money in the bank, but other people prefer to hide some money at home. Talk or write about all the places where you could hide money at home. Which place seems to make the most sense to you? Why?

Civil Servants

People who work for the government are called civil servants, but the word "civil" also means "to be polite," "to have good manners," "to be helpful," and "to be courteous." Talk or write about people whose job is to serve and help the public. Do they behave in a "civil" manner? How do they act? How should they act? Include specific details so that your listeners or readers know exactly what you mean.

"The Awful Fate of Melpomenus Jones"

Compare and contrast "My Financial Career" with another Stephen Leacock short story, "The Awful Fate of Melpomenus Jones." It is about a polite and timid young man who just could not bring himself to say goodbye. On the first day of his vacation, he went to visit friends, and somehow stayed and stayed, until, on the last day of his holiday, he finally departed in an unexpected way!

LIBRARY BOOKS

If you would like to read other works by Stephen Leacock, look for the following books in the class, school, or local library, or in a bookstore.

Literary Lapses
(Toronto: McClelland & Stewart, 1989)
A collection of short stories from which "My Financial Career" was taken. This edition features an afterword by Robertson Davies.

Arcadian Adventures with the Idle Rich
(Toronto: McClelland & Stewart, 1989)
A novel that looks at the lives of the wealthy in a large American city. This edition features an afterword by Gerald Lynch.

Feast of Stephen
(Toronto: McClelland & Stewart, 1990)
A collection of short pieces edited, with a long introduction, by Robertson Davies.

My Remarkable Uncle and Other Stories
(Toronto: McClelland & Stewart, 1992)
A collection of short pieces, with an afterword by James Doyle.

Sunshine Sketches of a Little Town
(Toronto: McClelland & Stewart, 1989)
A novel dealing with the business, politics, religion, and romance in a small Ontario town. This edition features an afterword by Jack Hodgins.

If you would like to read more about the life and work of Stephen Leacock, look for the following books in the class, school, or local library, or in a bookstore.

Leacock
A. F. Moritz and Theresa Moritz
(Toronto: Stoddart, 1985)
The most recent major biography of Leacock.

Remembering Leacock
Allan Anderson
(Ottawa: Deneau, 1983)
A collection of memories of Leacock by those who knew him.

Stephen Leacock
Robertson Davies
(Toronto: McClelland & Stewart, 1970)
A brief book of biography and criticism.

Stephen Leacock
James Doyle
(Toronto: ECW, 1992)
A short biography.

CHAPTER FOURTEEN

The Enchanted Caribou

retold by Elizabeth Cleaver

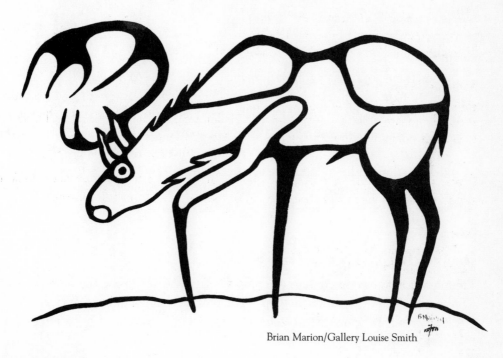

Brian Marion/Gallery Louise Smith

WARM-UP

Scanning Two Different Sources of Information

For this activity, you will quickly scan the summary of the story below and the story "The Fire Stealer" in Chapter Nine. After you read each statement below, decide if it is true or false. You do not need to find any other information as you read. Try to do the activity in less than three minutes.

1. Both legends took place a long time ago.
2. Nanabozho changed himself into a pine tree.

3. Tyya changed herself into a white caribou.
4. Nanabozho changed himself into a rabbit.
5. An evil shaman cast a spell on Tyya.
6. Nokomis cast a spell on Nanabozho.
7. Etosack killed a white caribou.
8. Nanabozho stole a torch from an old warrior.
9. The Inuit believe that white caribou are magic.
10. Both legends have a sad ending.

Summary

Long, long ago, a young maiden named Tyya wandered far from home and became lost in a thick fog. Etosack, a young caribou hunter, rescued her and took her to his tent. When Etosack left to go hunting the next day, he warned Tyya not to let anyone into the tent. But an evil shaman came and tricked her and cast a spell over her. Tyya was changed into a white caribou. Etosack despaired when he found her gone, but a dream told him how to use magic to change her back into a woman. That is why Inuit hunters are always kind to a white caribou — it might be an enchanted person.

Introduction to the Story

Think about these questions as you read the story: Why did the three brothers warn Tyya not to let anyone into the tent? How did the shaman change Tyya into a white caribou? How did Etosack change her back into a woman? Why are Inuit hunters kind to a white caribou?

The Enchanted Caribou

In the very earliest time, far away in a settlement by a northern lake, there lived a young woman called Tyya. She loved to wander alone collecting pieces of driftwood° and caribou° antlers° to make dolls for children. As she walked she sang to herself and watched the gulls° flap their wings in the clear air.

One day Tyya had wandered a long way from home when a heavy fog° descended and she could see nothing in front of her. Feeling lost and helpless, she sat down and wept°. After a few minutes something moved in the fog. Tyya was so frightened she stopped crying. The figure came closer and closer. Finally she could see what it was. A young man! When he spoke in a kindly voice, Tyya was no longer frightened. "What are you doing here?" he asked. "I was collecting driftwood when the fog descended," Tyya replied, "and I could see nothing in front of me. I am lost." "Don't worry," he said. "I live close by with my two brothers. My name is Etosack. Come with me."

Tyya followed Etosack to his house, a summer tent made of caribou hides°. She sat in front of a fire while Etosack served her caribou meat and broth° and fresh berries. After her meal she felt warm and contented. With Etosack beside her, she gazed happily into the fire and watched the shadows it cast on the wall of the tent. When the two brothers returned, they were surprised to find a beautiful woman sitting with Etosack. "Who is she?" asked the first brother. "How did she get here?" asked the second. "She was lost in the fog," Etosack replied, "and I asked her to stay with us until tomorrow. Her name is Tyya."

The three brothers were hunters of caribou that roamed the tundra° beyond the lake. Before lying down to sleep they performed a ceremonial dance to bring them success in the morning's hunt. First they put on caribou masks°, and coats and boots of caribou skin. Then, to make music for their dance, one of them got out his caribou-skin drum and started beating on it. While the brothers danced around the fire, their shadows flickering against the wall of their tent, they chanted a magic hunting song:

> ...caribou-bou-bou.
> Put your footprints on this land —
> this land I'm standing on
> is rich with the plant food you love.
> See, I'm holding in my hand
> the reindeer moss° you're dreaming of —
> so delicious, yum, yum, yum —
> Come, caribou, come.

Unable to resist the rhythmic drum beats, Tyya joined the brothers in their dance. The drumming quickened, and the dancing quickened with it. Tossing their arms in the air as they leapt around the fire, the four dancers whirled faster and faster until they fell to the ground exhausted.

In the morning, before they set out for the hunt, the three brothers warned Tyya not to let anyone into their tent while they were away. Left alone, Tyya took up a sharp knife and carved a piece of driftwood until a beautiful doll emerged. Then she made it a caribou-skin dress. While she sat working, someone came to the flap of the tent. "Let me in," said an old woman's voice, "and give me a drink of water." "I can't let you in," Tyya called. "This tent belongs to Etosack and his brothers. They have told me not to let anyone in while they are away." The old woman replied crossly°, "If you refuse to let me in, bad things will happen to you. I am a shaman°."

A shaman! Tyya knew that a shaman had supernatural powers and could do terrible things. She let the woman in, forgetting what the brothers had told her. After Tyya gave her a drink of water, the old woman said, "Now I will comb your hair," and she took out her magic ivory° comb. As she drew it through the tangles° in Tyya's hair, she started to sing:

Ajaja, aja, aja, jaja…

Tyya had never heard the melody before. It was so tender, so beautiful… She fell into a deep sleep, and the old woman crept away.

Tyya slept for many hours. When she woke and stretched her arms she felt herself being transformed. Antlers slowly sprouted° on her head, and her arms lengthened to legs. Her hands and feet became hooves°. She was no longer human.

Tyya had become a white caribou. It trotted° out of the tent and bounded across the tundra to join the herd°.

That evening, when the brothers returned, they found that Tyya had gone. "Why would she leave without telling us?" asked Etosack unhappily, for he had fallen in love with Tyya. That night Etosack had a dream about his dead grandmother, who had been a powerful shaman in her lifetime. She told him that Tyya had been changed into a white caribou by an evil shaman. "Do what I tell you and you will have her back. In the morning take a feather, the bone and sinew° of a caribou, a stone, and the doll that Tyya made. Then go out and look for the white caribou. When you find it, throw these things on its back and you will see what happens."

The next morning Etosack set out to find Tyya. He walked for many hours until he spotted a caribou herd in the distance. Coming closer to it, he saw what he was looking for: the white caribou. He ran towards the herd shouting joyfully, "Are you my Tyya, caribou-bou-bou?" When he reached the white animal, he threw the magic objects on its back.

Instantly the caribou changed into a woman. Into Tyya!

Etosack invited Tyya back to his tent and they lived together happily. His brothers put up a tent of their own nearby. Tyya still collected pieces of wood and antler for her dollmaking. Whenever she saw caribou, she thought of the time when she had been one of them, the most beautiful caribou in the herd. And ever since, when hunters meet a white caribou they treat it kindly and do not kill it, for it might be enchanted.

GLOSSARY

driftwood (n)   pieces of wood that are floating, driven along, or piled up under the force of wind, waves, or currents

caribou (n)   a type of North American reindeer

antlers (n)   the pair of branched horns of a male deer (stag) or other related animals, such as moose, elk, and caribou

gulls (n)   a largish flying seabird with a loud cry

fog (n)   very thick mist which makes it difficult to see

wept (v)   shed tears, cried

hides (n)   an animal's skin, especially when removed to be used for leather

broth (n)   soup in which meat, fish, rice, or vegetables have been cooked

tundra (n)   a cold, treeless plain in the far north of Europe, Asia, and North America

masks (n)   coverings for the face, to hide or protect it

moss (n)   a small, flat, green or yellow flowering plant that grows in a thick furry mass on wet soil or on a wet surface

crossly (adv)   angrily; in a bad-tempered way

shaman (n)   a person who has magical or enchanted powers

ivory (adj)   a hard white substance of which elephants' tusks are made

tangles (n)   a confused mass or disordered state of hair

sprouted (v)   grew or sent up new growth

hooves (n)   (or hoofs) the hard feet of certain animals, such as the horse

trotted (v)   moved at a fairly fast speed between a walk and a run

herd (n)   a group of animals of one kind that live and feed together

sinew (n)   a strong cord in the body connecting a muscle to a bone

There may be other words and expressions in the story that are not familiar to you. Write each one in your journal. Then look it up in a dictionary, ask another student, or ask the teacher for a definition. Write the definition on the line beside the word or expression. Try to use the new word or expression in a sentence.

READING ACTIVITY

Who?

You will probably want to look back and scan the text to decide on the answers to some of these questions. Discuss the answers with the teacher and other students.

1. Who got lost in the fog?
2. Who served caribou meat and broth for supper?
3. Who danced around the fire?
4. Who beat the drum?
5. Who warned Tyya not to let anyone into the tent?
6. Who made dolls for children out of driftwood?
7. Who combed Tyya's hair?
8. Who became a white caribou?
9. Who fell in love with Tyya?
10. Who told Etosack how to change the white caribou into a woman?
11. Who lived happily together?
12. Who treats white caribou kindly?

LISTENING ACTIVITY

The Inuit

Read the key words and the sentences below. First, listen to the text. Second, listen to the text and, in your journal, fill in the blanks with an appropriate word or expression from the list of key words. You will not use all the words. Third, listen to the text and complete the blanks. Discuss the answers with the teacher and other students.

Key Words

Alaska	Inuktitut
Arctic	Mackenzie
artistic	polar bears
Baffin Island	salmon
char	sculptures
Copper	seals
drawings	Ungava
Greenland	wall hangings
Inuit	walruses
Inuk	whales

1. The Inuit are the First Nations people who live along the _____ coast and islands of Canada.
2. The language of the Inuit is _____ .
3. _____ is an Inuktitut word meaning "the people."
4. A single member of this group is known as an _____ , meaning "one person."
5. _____ , caribou, muskoxen, _____ , and whales are among the most commonly hunted animals.
6. The most commonly caught fish are _____ , trout, and _____ .
7. The Inuit have a long _____ tradition.
8. Today, many Inuit support themselves by selling their _____ , prints, drawings, and _____ .
9. There are eight main Inuit groups in Canada: Baffin Island, Caribou, _____ , Iglulik, Labrador, Mackenzie, Netsilik, and _____ .
10. The Inuit are related to other aboriginal groups in _____ and Greenland.

DISCUSSION AND WRITING ACTIVITIES

Point of View

Imagine that you are Etosack or the shaman. From that point of view, retell the legend of "The Enchanted Caribou" either orally or in writing.

Inuit Legends

Have you ever heard or read about an Inuit legend? Talk or write about it with the teacher and other students. Then decide who has heard or read the most interesting one.

Create a Legend

Create your own legend about an animal that lives in a Northern climate. Here are some possibilities:

- the magic husky dogs
- the enchanted salmon
- the bewitched polar bear
- the phantom foxes

Share your legend with the teacher and other students. Then decide who has told or written the most memorable one.

The Inuit First Nations

Choose one of these Inuit groups: (1) Baffin Island, (2) Caribou, (3) Copper, (4) Iglulik, (5) Labrador, (6) Mackenzie, (7) Netsilik, or (8) Ungava.

Find out some information about the group, such as its history, territory, language, food, shelter, clothing, transportation, social and political organization, religion, art and leisure, or contemporary life.

Talk or write about the Inuit people that you have researched. In your opinion, what is the most interesting aspect of their culture?

LIBRARY BOOKS

If you would like to read other works by Elizabeth Cleaver, look for these books in the class, school, or local library, or in a bookstore.

The Enchanted Caribou
(Toronto: Oxford, 1985)
Illustrated by the author.

The Miraculous Hind
(Toronto: Holt Reinhart, 1973)
A Hungarian legend illustrated by the author.

If you would like to read more Inuit legends, look for the following books in the class, school, or local library, or in a bookstore.

Elik and Other Stories of the Mackenzie Eskimos
Herbert T. Schwartz
(Toronto: McClelland & Stewart, 1970)
A collection of short Inuit legends. Illustrated by Mona Ohoveluk.

Inuit Stories
Zebedee Nungak and Eugene Arima
(Ottawa: Canadian Museum of Civilization, 1988)
A collection of photographs of carvings accompanied by 46 Inuit legends told to the authors by the sculptors themselves.

More Tales from the Igloo
Agnes Nanogak
(Edmonton: Hurtig, 1986)
A collection of short Inuit legends. Illustrated by the author.

Tales from the Igloo
Maurice Metayer, editor
(Edmonton: Hurtig, 1972)
A collection of short Inuit legends. Illustrated by Agnes Nanogak.

CHAPTER FIFTEEN

Naomi's Road

JOY KOGAWA

Jack Long/National Archives of Canada (C–49271)

WARM-UP

Look at the picture carefully. This is an internment camp. You will read about a Japanese Canadian who spent some time there in the paragraph below.

Scanning

In this activity, you are asked to find the author's age, in years, at some of the major events in her life. For each of the following statements, write in your journal the author's age at the time the event took place. To do this, you will have to scan the brief biography of the author below and make calculations based on the information you find. Try to complete the entire activity in three minutes or less.

1. World War II began.   Age:
2. *The Splintered Moon* was published.   Age:
3. Her most popular work, *Obasan*, was published.   Age:
4. *Naomi's Road*, written for young adults, was published.   Age:
5. *Itsuku*, which continues the story of Naomi's life, was published.   Age:

Biography

Joy Kogawa was born in Vancouver in 1935. During World War II (1939-1945), she and her family were deported to an internment camp in the interior of British Columbia. Her first collection of poetry, *The Splintered Moon*, was published in 1968. Although she is considered primarily a poet, her most popular work is *Obasan* (1983), a semi-autobiographical novel about a child's experiences in a wartime internment camp. *Naomi's Road* (1986) covers much the same story, but is written for young adults. In 1992, Kogawa continued Naomi's life story with a second novel, *Itsuku* (1993).

Introduction to the Story

This selection is the sixth chapter of the novel *Naomi's Road*. Think about these questions as you read the chapter: What was Naomi's life like before this? How does she feel about the place where she lives now? Who is Obasan? Who is Stephen? Who is Uncle? Where are Naomi's parents? What happens to Naomi after this episode in her life?

Naomi's Road

Every morning I wake up in a narrow bunk bed° near the stove. I wish and wish we could go home. I don't want to be in this house of the bears° with newspaper walls. I want to be with Mama and Daddy and my doll in our real house. I want to be in my own room where the picture bird sings above my bed. And the real bird sings in the peach tree outside my bedroom window. But no matter how hard I wish, we don't go home.

The house is so crowded we can barely move around. In one small room there are two beds. One is for Obasan°. The other is for a long-faced° woman called Nomura-obasan. She's not well, Obasan says, and we must take care of her.

Daddy's sick too, Stephen says. His letters are from a hospital somewhere in the woods.

"When is he coming here?" I ask Obasan one night. We're sitting at the table after supper. The coal-oil lamp is on. "When will he get better?"

Nobody answers me. Nobody knows.

Stephen is practising his pieces on a folding cardboard° piano Daddy made. "The world is beautiful as long as there is music," Daddy wrote. "Keep the world beautiful, Stephen. If you listen hard you can hear all the notes."

Sometimes Stephen and I pretend we're at home again in our music room and the cardboard piano is real. We play guessing games and I have to guess which songs he's playing. Even if I'm older now, I like singing the kindergarten° songs the best.

Obasan is washing the supper dishes. She fills the basin from the water bucket° by the stove. "Plip" says the dipper° and "szt szt" goes the water as it spills on the hot stove. The box beside the stove is full of logs and kindling° wood. Obasan and Stephen chop the logs outside on a stump°.

Behind the house there's a path that goes up the mountain. If we climbed all the way we'd reach the sky. On our way up Stephen and I find tart° red strawberries the size of shirt buttons. And there are gooseberries, shiny and round as marbles. We find floppy° dark mushrooms too, growing on dead trees. Obasan will know if they're safe to eat. In early spring curly fiddleheads° poke out of the ground. They look like green question marks. We fill our jam pails and bring them all home to Obasan.

From a high rocky ledge° past a waterfall, we can see the world. Far below is the silvery river. And further away, rows and rows of little houses are tiny as toy blocks. Pencil-thin lines of smoke curl out of chimneys. Hundreds and hundreds of boys and girls like Stephen and me live in the toy block houses. Two families share each house and each family has one room. If you wanted to walk around you'd have to be as small as a doll.

In the spring and summer we all play outside. But then winter comes.

One cold day Stephen and I are playing outside. The minister and another man are carrying a cot° through the fluffy falling snow.

"For Uncle," the minister says when Stephen points to the cot.

"What?" Stephen interrupts excitedly. "Is Uncle coming here?"

When we get home, Obasan nods solemnly. "Yes, Uncle is coming tonight."

"Really?" I ask. "Is Daddy coming too? Can we go home?"

Nomura-obasan shakes her head sadly. "Not yet," she says.

"Come," Obasan says brightly. She wipes her hands on her apron. "There's so much to do. Just think! Uncle is on his way."

We're like elves° hopping about all afternoon. Obasan cooks the dried mushrooms and fiddleheads. I make paper decorations and paper baskets for jelly beans°. Even Nomura-obasan tries to help, but her hands are too shaky.

As we work, the snow keeps falling. The fence post looks like it's wearing a tall hat. Stephen puts his hand on the window to melt the frost so he can see. But after a while it gets dark.

At last we hear a stomp° stomp outside. Stephen throws the door open and in comes Uncle in a whoosh of snow.

"Uncle!" Stephen cries.

Uncle puts down his wooden box and sack and shakes the snow off his coat. His arms are wide as Papa Bear's. "Hello hello hello," he says as he lifts Stephen up.

Obasan takes off her apron. She folds her hands in front of her. "Welcome home," she says. "You are just in time."

Uncle looks at all the food and the decorations on the table. "Ah," he says, "it must be Christmas."

"You have come such a long way," Nomura-obasan says. She is sitting in bed and bows forward. Uncle bows as well and they both say, "It is such a long time."

Then he squats in front of me and scratches his head.

"And this big girl. Who can she be?" he asks. He's joking, of course, but I wonder if I've changed. He still looks the same.

He turns to his sack and takes out two wooden flutes°. With a whoop, Stephen leaps to Uncle. And then Stephen's fingers are dancing lightly over the smooth wood. At once the room fills with a bright dancing sound. Uncle slaps his knees as Stephen hops around and round the wooden box chairs. Stephen is like a rooster°, crowing with his head up high. He plays and plays.

"Oh there will be dancing," Nomura-obasan says, clapping her hands.

"You're just like your father," Uncle says, patting Stephen on the back. "Music all the time."

GLOSSARY

bunk bed (n)	one of two beds placed one above the other
house of the bears (exp)	reference to the fairy tale of Goldilocks and the Three Bears (Papa Bear, Mama Bear, and Baby Bear)
Obasan (n)	a Japanese term for aunt

long-faced (adj)	sad looking
cardboard (adj)	a thick, stiff paperlike material used for making boxes, the backs of books, etc.
kindergarten (n)	a school or class for children aged four to six which they attend usually for one year before entering grade school
water bucket (n)	an open metal, plastic, or wooden container with a handle for carrying liquids; pail
dipper (n)	a long-handled utensil for putting into a liquid for a moment
kindling (n)	materials for lighting a fire, especially dry wood, leaves, grass, etc.
stump (n)	the part of something left after the rest has been cut down, cut off, or worn down
tart (adj)	sharp to the taste; not sweet
floppy (adj)	soft and falling loosely
fiddleheads (n)	the small curled leaves of some ferns, eaten as a vegetable
ledge (n)	a flat shelf of rock
cot (n)	a light, narrow, usually single bed that folds flat and is easily carried
elves (n)	small fairies with pointed ears
jelly beans (n)	soft, sweet candies that come in different colours and flavours
stomp (n)	a loud heavy step
flutes (n)	pipelike wooden or metal musical instruments with finger holes, played by blowing across a hole in the side
rooster (n)	a fully grown male bird, especially a chicken

There may be other words and expressions in the chapter that are not familiar to you. Write each one in your journal. Then look it up in a dictionary, ask another student, or ask the teacher for a definition. Write the definition on the line beside the word or expression. Try to use the new word or expression in a sentence.

READING ACTIVITIES

Jigsaw Reading

What was Naomi's life like before this? Look at the summaries of Chapters 1 to 5 of *Naomi's Road* below. They are not in the proper sequence. Read them carefully and indicate which is first, second, third, and so on in your journal.

Chapter _____

Daddy has to go away. He tells Stephen and Naomi to be good and to listen to Obasan. She tells Stephen and Naomi that they're going away, too.

They take the train to the mountains. On the train there is a young woman with a baby. Obasan gives her some fruit, and an old woman gives her some cloth for a diaper.

Naomi plays with a ball and a Mickey Mouse toy. The dolls are tired, and so is Naomi. Obasan sings them a lullaby.

Chapter _____

Daddy, Mama, Stephen, and Naomi are at home one evening. Daddy teaches Stephen to play the piano. Mama sings the daffodil song to Naomi. At eight o'clock it's time for Naomi to go to bed.

Outside Naomi's bedroom window there is a peach tree. Mama tells her a story about a little boy who lives inside a giant peach and sings a song about the peach boy. Naomi wants to be a child forever.

Chapter _____

Mama doesn't come home from Japan. Daddy says she can't come home until the war is over. War is the worst and saddest thing in the world.

Stephen comes home crying. His glasses and his violin are broken. Naomi's doll is angry and starts to cry. War is stupid.

Naomi is frightened and wakes up at night. Daddy sings a funny song, but Naomi doesn't laugh. War is a terrible thing.

Chapter _____

Naomi plays with her dolls. She has a teddy bear, a toy mouse, a nurse doll, and a Japanese baby doll. Her friend Ralph plays with matches. He sets the curtains on fire, but Mama puts the fire out.

Mama goes to Japan to visit her great-grandmother who is sick. Obasan takes care of Stephen and Naomi. She doesn't understand English very well, but she is soft and gentle.

Chapter _____

The train stops at Slocan in the mountains. Obasan, Stephen, and Naomi get off. The train station is noisy and crowded. They leave with the minister and another man. Naomi starts to cry. She lost her doll! She left it on the train!

They walk into the woods. Stephen sees a small gray hut with tall weeds around it. It looks like the home of the three bears! It is very dusty inside and has newspaper walls.

Brainstorming

Brainstorm with the teacher and other students about what happens to Naomi after the episode in Chapter Six. What happens to Stephen, Obasan, Nomura-obasan, Uncle, Mother, and Father?

LISTENING ACTIVITY

A Letter from the Author

First, listen to the text. Second, listen to the text and fill in the blanks in your journal. Third, listen to the text and complete the blanks. Discuss the answers with the teacher and other students.

Dear Reader,

O Canada! What a vast, beautiful country. Here there are people from all around the world. And along with the Native Peoples, we are all Canadians together.

This little story is told by a Canadian child (1) _____ Naomi Nakane. She has black hair and lovely Japanese eyes and (2) _____ face like a valentine. Naomi's story happened in the (3) _____ before you were born, in the 1940s. In her (4) _____ there was a war going on. Canada and Japan were (5) _____. How sad that was. Suddenly she had to (6) _____ ashamed to be Japanese. She did not learn to (7) _____ or write Japanese and she tried to forget how (8) _____ speak Japanese. She never used chopsticks with strangers.

It (9) _____ hard to understand, but Japanese Canadians were treated as enemies (10) _____ home, even though we were good Canadians. Not one Japanese Canadian (11) _____ ever found to be a traitor to our (12) _____. Yet our cameras and cars, radios and fishing (13) _____ were taken away. After that our homes and (14) _____ and farms were also taken and we were (15) _____ to live in camps in the mountains. Fathers (16) _____ older brothers and uncles were made to work (17) _____ roads in the Rocky Mountains. If you ever drive through (18) _____ beautiful mountains, you may ride over some roads (19) _____ by Japanese Canadians.

Naomi's road is a different kind of (20) _____. It is the path of her life. If you walk with her a while, you will find the name of a very important road.

DISCUSSION AND WRITING ACTIVITIES

"What Do I Remember of the Evacuation?" by Joy Kogawa

Read the following poem as many times as you wish. Compare and contrast *Naomi's Road* with the poem. Talk or write about your responses with the teacher and other students.

What Do I Remember of the Evacuation?

What do I remember of the evacuation?
I remember my father telling Tim and me
About the mountains and the train
And the excitement of going on a trip.
What do I remember of the evacuation?
I remember my mother wrapping
A blanket around me and my
Pretending to fall asleep so she would be happy
Though I was so excited I couldn't sleep
(I hear there were people herded
Into the Hastings Park like cattle.
Families were made to move in two hours
Abandoning everything, leaving pets
And possessions at gun point.
I hear families were broken up
Men were forced to work. I heard

It whispered late at night
That there was suffering) and
I missed my dolls.
What do I remember of the evacuation?
I remember Miss Foster and Miss Tucker
Who still live in Vancouver
And who did what they could
And loved the children and who gave me
A puzzle to play with on the train.
And I remember the mountains and I was
Six years old and I saw a giant
Gulliver of Gulliver's Travels scanning the horizon
And when I told my mother she believed it too
And I remember how careful my parents were
Not to bruise us with bitterness

And I remember the puzzle of Lorraine Life
Who said "Don't insult me" when I
Proudly wrote my name in Japanese
And Tim flew the Union Jack
When the war was over but Lorraine
And her friends spat on us anyway
And I prayed to the God who loves
All the children in his sight
That I might be white.

A Letter to Joy Kogawa

In Joy Kogawa's letter to the readers of *Naomi's Road*, she wrote statements such as these:

O Canada! What a vast, beautiful country. Here there are people from all around the world. And along with the Native Peoples, we are all Canadians together.

Naomi's road is a different kind of road. It is the path of her life. If you walk with her a while, you will find the name of a very important road.

Read these statements carefully and think about them. Write a letter to Joy Kogawa about one or both of these statements.

LIBRARY BOOKS

If you would like to read other stories and poems by Joy Kogawa, look for the following books in the class, school, or local library, or in a bookstore.

Naomi's Road
(Toronto: Oxford, 1986)
The novel from which this chapter was taken. We strongly encourage you to read the whole story.

A Choice of Dreams
(Toronto: McClelland & Stewart, 1974)
A collection of short poems, half of which concern Japan.

Itsuku
(Toronto: Penguin, 1993)
Continues Naomi's story as an adult in a novel written for adults.

Jericho Road
(Toronto: McClelland & Stewart, 1978)
The author's most recent book of poetry.

Obasan
(Toronto: Penguin, 1983)
The story of Naomi's experiences in the internment camp, written for adults.

If you would like to read more about the internment of Canadians during World War II, look for these books in the class, school, or local library, or in a bookstore.

A Child in Prison Camp
Shizuye Takashima
(Montreal: Tundra, 1971)
A book about the author's memories of her time in an internment camp. Written for young adults with illustrations by Takashima.

Dangerous Patriots
William Pepka and Kathleen M. Pepka
(Vancouver: New Star, 1983)
An account of Canadians who were interned because of their political beliefs during World War II.

The Enemy that Never Was
Ken Adachi
(Toronto: McClelland & Stewart, 1991)
A book dealing with the experiences of interned Japanese Canadians, before and after World War II. Written for adults, this revised edition features an introduction by Timothy Findley and an afterword by Roger Daniels.

The Politics of Racism
Ann Gomer Sunahara
(Toronto: Lorimer, 1981)
A book dealing with the internment of Japanese Canadians.

Within the Barbed Wire Fence
Takeo Ujo Nakano
(Toronto: University of Toronto, 1980)
A Japanese man's account of his internment during World War II.

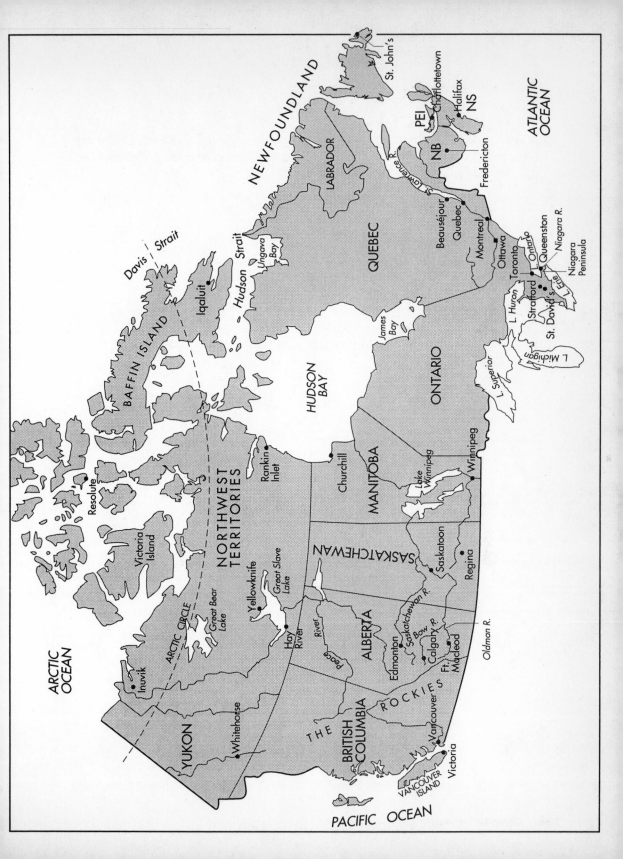